HEROES

HEROES

Shaping Lives through Family and Culture

STEFFEN T. KRAEHMER

Fairview Press   *Minneapolis*

Published by Fairview Press, 2450 Riverside Avenue South, Minneapolis, MN 55454.

Library of Congress Cataloging-in-Publication Data

Kraehmer, Steffen T.
      Heroes : shaping lives through family and culture / by Steffen T. Kraehmer
          p. cm.
      Includes bibliographical references and index.
      ISBN 0-925190-77-2 (hardcover : acid free)
      1. Parent and teenager. 2. Parenting. 3. Teenagers—Attitudes. 4. Role models. 5. Heroes. 6. Social values. I Title.
HQ799.15.K73 1995
649'.125—dc20   95-22641

First Printing: September 1995

Printed in the United States of America
99 98 97 96 95   7 6 5 4 3 2 1

Cover design: Circus Design

Publisher's Note: Fairview Press publishes books and other materials related to the subjects of physical health, mental health, and family issues. Its publications, including *Heroes,* do not necessarily reflect the philosophy of Fairview Hospital and Healthcare Services or their treatment programs.

For a free current catalog of Fairview Press titles, please call this toll-free number: 1-800-544-8207.

This book is dedicated to you and the many other parents who struggle, sacrifice, and surrender yourselves to setting a good example for your children. You are heroes in the strongest sense of the word. You are courageous, honest, kind, and committed to being positive role models for your child and others. I am honored to dedicate this book to each and every one of you. Congratulations and thank you for being today's true heroes.

Contents

Acknowledgments

I would like to extend my appreciation and thanks to:

Ed Wedman, Publisher, Fairview Press,
Jay Hanson, Editor, Fairview Press,
Julie Odland, Editor, Fairview Press,

Jack Caravela for getting this project started,

Pat Samples for providing wonderful editing suggestions and ongoing professional support,

Sheri Harlan for her persistent and sincere inquiries regarding the deadlines for this book,

Sharon Johnson for assistance in proofreading the galleys,

Annette Covatta for her spiritual encouragement while writing this book,

Inga Pellegrino for sharing insights on parenting teenagers,

and to my wife, Sue, and two sons, Zachary and Ryan, for being a significant part of my life and understanding the times I expressed that "I really do need to work on this *Heroes* book."

Introduction

"The child says nothing but what is heard by the fire."
—Author Unknown

What a great vacation! We were enjoying six days in Cape May, New Jersey—on the beach, in the pool and visiting the sights. I remember my older son, Ryan, closely observing my behavior during the entire week. As usual, I joked around a lot, and he watched this very intently. I also laughed a lot, even chuckled at my own puns and clever statements once in a while. Ryan inquired regularly, "What are you laughing about?" By the end of the week, he was mimicking my behavior, telling his own funny one-liners and riddles. Even though I knew it all too well, it hit me "right between the eyes"—I was Ryan's role model.

Ryan is curious about people's behavior and the world around him. He is an imitator, especially of adults, and he is entering the "hero worship" stage. I began to ponder on who might capture his interest, who he might idolize. I wondered, "Who are the heroes of this generation?" I knew at this point I was going to research this subject and be ready for this important stage in my son's life. Like my previous book, *Quantity Time*, I would create, as one reporter described, a "master plan" for spending time with your child. Now I was going to prepare a comprehensive report on adolescence and heroes. It was imperative.

At the same time, one of America's well-known celebrities,

1

O. J. Simpson, was making headline news. People, young and old, were shocked. Could one of their heroes have murdered two people? And there were other celebrities who also had made negative headlines in the recent past—Michael Jackson, Jennifer Capriati, Tonya Harding, River Phoenix, Mike Tyson, even Princess Diana. Some event in their lives marred their images, and many people were disillusioned. Among the disillusioned were many, many of our youth. When their heroes and role models disappoint them, young people get depressed, angry, even suicidal.

Celebrities and sports stars become idols and role models for many teens. Youth worship these idols in ways that confuse and disrupt their upbringing. Celebrities have a hypnotic power. It is a powerful energy that can be constructive—or destructive. It is a power comparable to fire. Fire is intriguing, especially to youngsters. Fire, when used properly, is useful and beautiful but, when used incorrectly or when out of control, is deadly!

Shortly after the O. J. Simpson occurrence, another major event took place. Woodstock '94 drew over 350,000 youth to Saugerties, New York. These young people, many still in high school, were determined to claim their own place in the cultural zeitgeist. The event was supposed to be a weekend of music, peace, and alliance, but for many it was three long days of mud, money, and misery.

Living so close to the site of Woodstock 94, I ventured to the site one week after its conclusion. The aftermath stunned me. It was a dump—a landfill—a discharge of mud, garbage, personal belongings, human waste, and leftover Pepsi products. What I saw bothered me, especially as I thought about the activities our young people either witnessed or participated in during these three days in August: sneaking into the compound, drinking, taking drugs, having sex, and stealing food and soda.

I thought about why this event was organized. Nostalgia? No, this was not the sixties any more, and Woodstock '94 was not even taking place at the original site. Money? Perhaps.

I also thought about why the people came to this affair. A

reunion? No, the majority of those attending this event probably were not even born in 1969! A time of celebration? Perhaps.

I pondered these two questions for many weeks. I conclud-
ed that for many it was definitely a search. They were on a
quest to find camaraderie, a massive summer party, or maybe
an entertainer they might think of as a hero. For other individuals it was an opportunity to emulate what was done 25 years
earlier by "now adults" who had been boasting about their
1969 historic event for years.

Within the same time period, a fourth event took place
relating to the topic of heroes. My publisher, Fairview Press,
wanted me to research and prepare a manuscript on parents
seeking heroes. Fairview Press is interested in the well-being
and growth of families and I knew if they were pursuing this
topic, it must be of interest to many, many parents. Since I was
researching this information for my own parenting experience,
I could prepare it for others. I knew this would be a worthy
task.

I dove into this project and found it extremely exciting.
Researching and organizing information are my forte. This
would be a real treat to explore the subject of heroes and share
my findings with so many others. One of the most intriguing
aspects about this investigation was that I uncovered a lot of
good news regarding raising children in this seemingly confusing and negative world. First of all, it became apparent that
we, as parents, do have quite a bit of say-so in how our children grow up, including the shaping of their values and
morals. Celebrities and athletes may have a strong influence
and might be described as the flame or torch, but WE AS PARENTS
ARE THE REAL FIRE. We are the example our children look to and
follow. What we say and do is extremely powerful, more than
we sometimes realize.

Another important way that we can guide our children in
this area is by interpreting what is taking place in the world of
heroes—the celebrities, sports stars, and other famous people
we see on television and in the news. We can select and present
positive role models and, at the same time, discuss the humanness and sometimes downfall of today's superstars.

Many of today's heroes are Hollywood or sports stars, but many are not. These non-celebrity heroes are everywhere but you have to be on the lookout for them in everyday life. One of our responsibilities as parents is to identify these individuals and their "heroic" accomplishments or traits. We need to take a deeper look at these heroes, analyze what they've done, and communicate this to our child. These everyday heroes are people who demonstrate such qualities as charity, leadership, courage, perseverance, devotion, compassion, and commitment. And literally, these people come from all walks of life and all ages.

One of the bravest individuals I knew was a 12-year-old girl named Tricia. I was acquainted with her through the Make-A-Wish program. Tricia had only one lung and rested much of the time. Her special bed at home had a large tank of oxygen next to it, in case she needed it. When I visited her home to discuss the plans for her family to visit Disney World, she was extremely happy. As plans progressed, she became more and more excited and talked about buying Mickey Mouse souvenirs for her whole family. Although she grew weaker and weaker, she made the trip. Her dream came true. She had a vision and pursued it with enthusiasm. She did it in a way that made others smile. People liked to be around her, and I was one of her biggest fans. Tricia was a caring person who loved vanilla ice cream, Doritos, and life. For me, Tricia was a special hero indeed. Why? Because I admired her for her simplicity, charm, and love of life. Being around Tricia changed me. I learned how to appreciate little things like ice cream and Doritos and the big things like life itself.

We need heroes, whether they be famous people or our next door neighbor. They help us define ourselves and help us grow, as individuals and as a society. As parents, we need to understand more about heroism and role modeling and how to best present them to our children. This aspect of parenting has a synergistic effect, providing both an aid to the positive development of your child and an affirmative steppingstone toward fulfilling your role as a caring, responsible parent. This is your opportunity for a win-win venture with your child.

I'm presenting this book to you as an aid to make the most of your child's adolescent years. This is a special time for your child. Ryan Hollady, the 11-year-old author of the recent book, *What Preteens Want Their Parents To Know*, shares this advice to parents in his introduction:

"This is an important time for us (going from being a little kid to teenager). We only travel this road together once. Let's make the most of it."

"There are two ways of spreading light; to be a candle, or the mirror that reflects it."
                    —Edith Wharton (1862–1937)
                    U.S. Novelist and Poet

SECTION 1

Parents, You Are the Light— A Candle

Hundreds of them are in every community. They are everywhere—heroes, that is. The nineties seem to be the decade of the hero.

The media have become fascinated with labeling large numbers of individuals as heroes.

Shot down over Bosnia, Captain Scott O'Grady spent six days living off bugs and rainwater, and was then rescued and nationally proclaimed an American Hero. *Newsweek* presents a cover story presenting achievement awards to "Everyday Heroes." And the film industry creates Pocahontas and Batman as fantasy heroes for our youth.

If one looks at the extended span of a child's life, these individuals and characters are sparks that will flicker for only a short time. Today and into the next millennium, society contains individuals that are illuminating flames in the lives of our children. They are powerful. They are the driving force in facilitating the growth of our youth. They are the number one hero and role model today. Who are these people?

Section 1 offers an in-depth look at the most important people in a child's life—parents. You will be introduced to a new hero description and five major insights every parent, teacher, politician—every adult, should become familiar with.

An organization known as the Christophers has the motto: "It is better to light one candle than to curse the darkness." Through this book, I hope you accept the challenge to be the candle—the light—in your child's life, burning ever so brightly for your child to see. And through your heroism the shaping of a life will take place through family and culture.

Note: A helpful appendix worksheet for each chapter appears at the end of the book. You may want to refer to the appropriate form after reading each chapter. The appendixes begin on page 238.

1

Understand Who Your Child's # 1 Hero and Role Model Is

True heroes are rare in today's world. And all too often, those who are really making a difference in our communities go unnoticed and unrewarded.
—President Bill Clinton

Heroes. The term is paradoxical, mystical, dangerous, yet very important in our lives. Historically the word has signified an individual who performed an exceptional achievement for a higher purpose—a dedicated soldier or a brave firefighter. But recently hero has been interchanged with words like celebrity or superstar, often referring to a movie idol or prominent athlete.

The word can have contradictory meanings, depending on who uses it. To military veterans, for example, a hero might mean a military conqueror, one who has killed others or masterminded a military plan to overthrow another government or country. To people working in rescue professions, by contrast, hero means one who has performed a courageous, life-saving act.

The concept of heroes is obscure. Some heroes, such as Babe Ruth, become legends, while others, such as Donald Trump, come and go. In addition, some people are only recognized as heroes after they are dead, such as the artist Michelangelo or the musician Beethoven, while others such as Forrest Gump seem to appear instantly or may not even be real at all.

Today's heroes, often described to your child as celebrities or idols, are causing concern to many parents. Parents feel that the poor example set by these individuals is ruining their children's lives. Parents see their children envy and imitate the negative behavior of these celebrities.

But heroes are needed in our lives. They provide a sense of wonderment, act as role models, inspire us, and perform extraordinary deeds.

As we think about this uncertain cliché, "hero," let's determine how we might picture a hero by looking at these true-life situations and individuals. For each one, consider these questions:

• Who is the hero (if there is one)? Why?

• What are the outstanding characteristics of this individual that makes him or her a hero?

Who is the hero?

General Norman Schwarzkopf, supreme commander of the allied forces in the Persian Gulf War . . . or Air Force Colonel David W. Eberly, former POW whose F-15E fighter jet was shot down over Iraq . . . or are the real heroes, as Colonel David proclaimed, "the folks back home who had stood behind, and prayed for, the troops"?

Who is the hero?

Bree Walker, television anchorwoman with a deformity called ectrodactylism . . . or her daughter who was also born with this "handicap". . . or the mother I recently saw in the supermarket parking lot pushing her disabled twin daughters in wheelchairs . . . or the twin girls?

Who is the hero?

Doctor Benjamin S. Carson, Director of Pediatric Neurosurgery at the Johns Hopkins University School of Medicine in Baltimore, Maryland, who was the primary surgeon in the dramatic and successful 22-hour operation separating the West German Siamese twins joined at the head . . . or Karen Fox who dresses up as Raggedy Ann and visits hospital patients and comforts them?

Who is the hero?

John Testrake from Richmond, Missouri, Captain of TWA Flight 847 that was hijacked in the Mediterranean with 14 passengers on board and kept captive for 17 days . . . or the airline mechanic who found Tabitha, a three-year-old, brown-and-white cat that had spent 12 days and 32,000 miles wandering around the fuselage of a Boeing 747 . . . or the owner, Carol Ann Timmel, who persisted in giving more time to search for the cat?

Who is the hero?

Nelson Mandela, President of South Africa . . . or Alice Chu, a claims representative for the Supplemental Security Income Program in Flushing, New York, who positions herself as an expert on Social Security issues for the Chinese-American community?

Who is the hero?

David Koresh, cult leader killed in Waco, Texas . . . or the four FBI agents who were killed storming the facility . . . or Paul Hill who killed an abortion clinic doctor and his escort in Pensacola, Florida . . . or the judge and jury who sentenced him?

Who is the hero?

Neil Alden Armstrong, first human to set foot on the moon on July 20, 1969 . . . or Christa McAuliffe, a New Hampshire teacher, and the six astronauts who were killed moments after the space shuttle Challenger exploded on January 28, 1986?

Who is the hero?

Mariah Carey, Madonna, Cher, Gloria Estefan, or Amy Grant . . . or Michael Jackson, one of the Rolling Stones, Elton John, or Elvis Presley . . . or maybe even Elvis Presley's daughter, Lisa Marie Presley, and Michael Jackson as a married couple?

Who is the hero?

Charles Barkley, a professional basketball player, who doesn't want to be a role model . . . or Joe Montana, four-time Super Bowl quarterback . . . or Nancy Lopez, champion golfer who was inducted into the World Golf Hall of Fame in 1989 . . . or Dennis Byrd, the New York Jets leading lineman who broke his neck and lay paralyzed on the playing field, yet made a miraculous recovery . . . or Roberto Clemente, a famous baseball player who died in a plane crash while bringing aid to earthquake victims in Nicaragua . . . or the legendary baseball player Babe Ruth . . . or tennis star Arthur Ashe?

Who is the hero?

Arnt Gulbrandsen, a 25-year-old Norwegian computer programmer who used a "cancelbot" to stop a Phoenix law firm from advertising on Usenet . . . or Alabamian Heather Whitestone, Miss America 1995, who doctors said would never go beyond the third grade . . . or Robert Lambert, a 15-year-old Boy Scout from Burnsville, Minnesota, who saved a two-year-old girl's life by performing CPR . . . or Evan, an 11-year-old boy from Ontario, Canada, facing up to a dysfunctional cycle in his family?

Who is the hero?

The eight Blomstom children who were adopted into different families after their parents were killed . . . or the Clinton family . . . or your family?

Well, who are the heroes? Did you come up with certain characteristics that are needed to be classified a hero?

In a nationwide poll of 1,006 adults, 58% said they had had a role model in their childhood. Think about your childhood. Did you have a hero? Who was it? Why? And who is your child idolizing? Why?

Take a minute or two and write your own definition of a hero. This is important as we search for our child's heroes.

A hero is _____

_____

_____

Today many types of people are called heroes including soldiers, rescue workers, celebrities, athletes, historical figures, mythological characters, Good Samaritans, and mentors. People identify these different groups as heroes for a variety of reasons. Someone who has been protected by military personnel or rescued by fire fighters obviously is grateful for this life-saving deed and sees those responsible as heroes. Celebrities are labeled heroes for their popularity, stardom, and financial success. Athletes are admired for their ability, media attention, and also financial status. Historical figures come to be known as heroes for their leadership or bravery. Mythological characters usually have a mystique surrounding them and offer a spiritual lesson. Good Samaritans, like life-savers, have automatically been seen as quiet heroes. And mentors are heroes because they have dynamic personalities or have accomplished extraordinary things.

Are all of these groups of people heroes? Let's continue our search for a description of hero by consulting four "experts."

Merriam Webster's Collegiate Dictionary defines hero as "a mythological or legendary figure often of divine descent endowed with great strength or ability; an illustrious warrior; a man (or woman) admired for his or her achievements and noble qualities; or one that shows great courage."[1] Okay, pretty basic dictionary jargon. How about something a little more in-depth?

Rollo May, well-known psychologist and author, tries to help us understand the importance of heroes in this way: "The rediscovery of heroism is central to the regaining of our myths and the arising of new myths that will suffice to inspire us to go beyond the cocaine, the heroin, the depressions and the suicides, through the inspiration of myths that lift us above a purely mundane existence."[2]

Joseph Campbell, author, teacher and philosopher summarizes his extensive research on heroism by these statements. "A hero or heroine is someone who has found or achieved or done something beyond the normal range of achievement and experience. A hero is someone who has given his (or her) life to someone bigger than himself (or herself) or other than himself (herself)."[3]

And the inspirational author Arthur Gordon shares his favorite definition of a hero: "A hero is someone who is to be cherished not so much for what they have accomplished in their own lives, but for what they have accomplished in mine, for how they have inspired me to grow and to change and to become more of what I was created to be."[4]

Let's analyze and expand on Gordon's concept of a hero as someone who inspires you to grow and change and become more of what you were created to be. First I want to confirm that the "basic" hero is a person who saves a life. In fact, *hero* comes from the Greek word "to protect." That train of thinking will always exist because saving a life is an extremely noble act. But for someone to label as a hero a person who has not saved a life, not only must the heroic deed be spectacular, but it must have helped that someone grow in some significant way. Heroes perform deeds that provide a significant, positive change in another person. Let me say that again. A "real" hero performs a deed that provides a meaningful, positive change in someone (and we want that person to be your child).

Since we are focusing on our children, let's center on the most significant hero in your child's life. If you think of one individual that impresses your child the most and can be labeled a hero, it is definitely YOU!

You are the figure endowed with great strength and ability who shows great courage (Webster). You inspire your child to go beyond mundane existence (May). You have done something beyond the normal range of achievement and experience, giving to someone other than yourself (Campbell). And you accomplish growth and change in another person—your child (Gordon). You are your child's hero. Yes, you really are!

Parents are the highest level of heroes. Going back to the basic notion of a hero being a life-saver, a parent far exceeds that definition. First, parents are life-givers—the most extraordinary of human experiences. Parents are life-savers—we protect our infants and toddlers from harm and illness. And parents are life-raisers, providing guidance and unconditional love for a lifetime. Yes, that certainly describes the mightiest of heroes.

Jan Blaustone, author of *The Joy of Parenthood* and *Every Family Is Special*, makes this statement:

"No matter how many years go by, he (or she) will always be your little pumpkin, and you'll always be his (or her) biggest hero."

In the demanding and complex role of parent, I've found it helpful to have a few basic foundational concepts I can focus on each day. There are five major insights that I would like to share with you. You can use them to help you focus your energies as a parent. Here is the first one:

Understand who your child's #1 hero and role model is—you!

A number of national studies and surveys centering on the subject of heroes clearly back up the above statement, and what makes this research so convincing is that it is taken from the youth's point of view. The most recent of these studies was done by the Children's Defense Fund:

"CDF-sponsored focus groups with Black and Latino 13- to 15-year-olds in Atlanta, Washington, D.C., and Orange County,

California revealed a powerful message regarding the key role that parents continue to play in the lives of adolescents. **The youths said they consider their parents and other adult family members to be the most powerful influence on them—more important than friends, television, and other media."**[5] I've highlighted this revelation for you to read and read again.

This in itself is wonderful news, but a second part of this study points out the following interesting notion: "When other focus groups composed of the parents of minority teenagers were asked to assess their influence on their children, they said they saw themselves as having a very limited effect on their children's values and actions, **which suggests that parents are underestimating the potential impact of strong guidance."**[6] Again I'm emphasizing this deduction.

Yes, you as a parent are a hero. You are extremely important in your child's life. Our youth believe this, now it is your turn to be convinced and acknowledge this truth.

Here's just a sampling of what today's youth are saying about parents as heroes from a Gallup Poll commissioned by *USA Today* and CNN:

> "My dad is the most significant male in my life. He grew up poor, the youngest of eight on a farm, and he went on to get a college degree."
>
> Alex Bass, 14, Raleigh, North Carolina

> "My mother worked, and my father had his own business. He was the one who picked me up at school. And he brought me up to believe girls should have the same opportunities as boys."
>
> Evelin Nagy, 16 Encinitas, California

> "I think athletes are good role models, especially Magic Johnson, who has really tried to help others. But it's Mom and Dad who are always there for me."
>
> Rachel Hegburg, 15, Exeter, Rhode Island

"My mother lived in a teeny, tiny town in Pennsylvania, and lived so poor. But she made the best of it and moved on, graduated from college, got a better life. I just think that is neat."

Emalie Huriaux, 15, San Ramon, California

"My dad is most influential in my life. I have many of his mannerisms, speech patterns, vocabulary. I have his same outlook."

Matthew Otteman, 16, Omaha, Nebraska

"I really respect both my parents. They have strong beliefs, morals and stuff, and they are really successful."

Amy Frost, 14, Laramie, Wyoming[7]

Here are the results from other research, completed in the last five years, that directly reported the opinions of youth:

• RespecTeen in Minneapolis, Minnesota, a multi-million-dollar program helping parents and teenagers work together to surmount the challenges of adolescence, announced that "research has shown that, in most cases, families influence teenagers more than any other single entity."[8]

• The Eastman Kodak company surveyed 21,000 fourth-grade students in 44 cities. Guess the results of this multiple-choice question, "Who is the number one hero of America's 9- and 10-year olds"?

a. Bart Simpson
b. George Bush
c. Paula Abdul
d. Bo Jackson
e. None of the above

The children overwhelmingly filled in their own selections and named their own parents as heroes, with their teachers coming in second. Sports star Bo Jackson was third; others were barely mentioned.

• In a private survey by author Bill Sanders of 7,500 teens in the seventh through twelfth grades, the direct question, "Who are your heroes?" was asked.

33. 1% selected parents, dad or mom.
31. 1% selected athletes/sports stars
14. 9% selected friends
11. 0% selected siblings
10. 2% selected actors/actresses[9]

• Group Publishing asked hundreds of teenagers "What do you think most influences today's teenagers about what's right and wrong?" (Teenagers could choose more than one category.)

50% said parents
31% said kids' own experiences
23% said church and youth group
23% said friends[10]

• 1,500 schoolchildren were asked, "What do you think makes a happy family?"
Social scientists Nick Stinnett and John DeFrain report that children "did not list money, cars, fine homes, or televisions." Instead the answer most frequently offered was "doing things together."[11]

• Holiday Inn advertises its hotels by placing a full page ad in major magazines using this headline:

89% OF KIDS WOULD LIKE TO SPEND MORE TIME WITH THEIR PARENTS.

Criteria for parent as hero

You are the most powerful influence on your child. Your children not only see you as a hero but want to be with you. What a wonderful affirmation! What a tremendous accomplishment for you. You should feel good about this. Just think, YOU ARE A HERO! Today's youth are saying this over and over again; likewise this statement is backed by almost every family professional. I want to repeat this again and again—you are the most significant and most powerful influence on your child's behavior and values. YOU ARE THE FIRE.

Welcome to this distinguished group known as heroes, but realize that being a hero is not easy. It is a big responsibility. And not all parents are heroes.

A parents' group created this classified ad for the position of PARENT, which I would rename HERO.

24 hours per day, 365 days per year position available. No vacations, no pay. Duties unpredictable. Benefits intangible.

Must be loving, yet firm; organized yet flexible; mature, but young enough to possess unlimited energy. Sense of humor an asset.

Minimum qualifications: degrees in psychology, child development, education, nursing, and management. Additional training helpful. Must possess valid driver's license.

Parenting is an extraordinarily difficult, time-consuming, and thankless task but indeed heroic. I've identified 20 criteria for the parent as hero. They are:

1. You accept the responsibility.
2. You take care of your children.
3. You provide the moral example.
4. You set basic values.
5. You model positive behavior when dealing with difficulties.
6. You show your child is important.
7. You meet the challenge.
8. You are the right kind of hero.
9. You admit your imperfection.

10. You treat your child with respect.
11. You will be imitated by your child in all you do.
12. You change your behavior as needed.
13. You are self-disciplined.
14. You have a significant role.
15. You are a role model.
16. You have the most lasting effect.
17. You build your child's self-esteem and your family connectedness.
18. You form the world.
19. You shape the future.
20. You love your child.

Let's see how the experts are substantiating my list of traits for parent as hero.

1. You accept the responsibility. "No job can compete with the responsibility of shaping and molding a new human being."
—Dr. James C. Dobson
Founder and President, Focus on the Family

2. You take care of your children. "We all ought to be trying to make the world a better place, but people don't want to talk about that anymore. That's what I've been doing all these years—showing parents that if they would take care of their little people, we would have a lot less trouble in this world."
—Dr. Leila Denmark
96 Year-old Practicing Pediatrician

3. You provide the moral example. "The single most powerful teaching tool is parental example, and this is perhaps truer in the moral area than in any other."
—Dr. William Mitchell & Dr. Charles Paul Conn
Authors, *The Power of Positive Parenting*

4. You set basic values. "The family is the most basic unit of government. As the first community to which a person is attached and the first authority under which a person learns to live, the family establishes society's most basic values."

—Charles Colson
Author, Watergate Participant

5. You model positive behavior when dealing with difficulties. "Give them a good model. The way you handle your own problems and frustrations will provide a model for your children."

—Michael H. Popkin, Ph. D.
Founder and President, Active Parenting

6. You show your child is important. "Children want two things. They want to believe their parents are okay and they want to matter."

—John Bradshaw
Author, *Bradshaw On: The Family*

7. You meet the challenge. "Children will invariably talk, eat, walk, think, respond, and act like their parents. Give them a target to shoot at. Give them a goal to work toward. Give them a pattern that they can see clearly, and you give them something that gold and silver cannot buy."

—Billy Graham
World Religious Leader

8. You are the right kind of hero. "The second age of childhood is the age of imitation, which occurs between the ages of eight and twelve. During these years, role models are most important to a child. Rules are important, but example is the great stimulus.

The next age is the age of inspiration—ages thirteen and up. He must have heroes. If he is not given heroes, he will find them; if he is not inspired by the right kind of heroes, he will be inspired by the wrong kind."

—Zig Ziglar, Motivational Speaker
Author, *Raising Positive Kids in a Negative World*

9. You admit your imperfection. "I think your family is your best teacher. To me, family means sharing inadequacies, imperfections, and feelings with each other, and still loving each other.

If you have a child at home, make sure that child knows that you are imperfect."
> —Dr. Bernie S. Siegel
> Author, *How To Live Between Office Visits*

10. You treat your child with respect. "Every concept we have of who we are, we had to learn while we were growing up. When a child is born, he has an extraordinarily high need for love and touching. A child learns whether or not he is lovable or worthwhile or intelligent or talented by the way he is treated by his parents."
> —Brian Tracy, Motivational Speaker
> Author, *The Psychology of Achievement* (tape)

11. You will be imitated by your child in all you do. "The best way to influence your kids' values is to model those values you think important. Kids accept the values they respect from people they like. They'll imitate their parents in everything from the way they lift a fork to the way they vote."
> —Dr. Thomas Gordon
> Founder of Parent Effectiveness Training (PET)

12. You change your behavior as needed. The child's behavior can most effectively be influenced by changing your own behavior. Responsible children are influenced by responsible parents."
> —Don Dinkmeyer and Gary D. McKay
> Founders, STEP (Systematic Training For
> Effective Parenting)

13. You are self-disciplined. "If a child sees his parents day in and day out living without self-restraint or self-disci-

pline, then he will come in the deepest fibers of his being to believe that that is the way to live."
        —Dr. M. Scott Peck
        Psychiatrist, Author

14. You have a significant role. "And what children most need are parents who are significant in their lives. Parents are their children's primary role models. Children learn from us and imitate our behavior, whether we like it or not. We learn to be humans by watching other humans behave, and children learn human values by watching their parents—how they talk to each other, how they handle moral dilemmas, how they take responsibility for their choices, how they treat their own parents, how honestly, or dishonestly, they deal with the facts of their own lives."
        —Dr. Lee Salk
        Author, *Familyhood*

15. You are a role model. "The best thing we can do for our children is to consciously work at being role models for them."
    —Og Mandino
    World-Renowned Inspirational and Self-Help Author

16. You have the most lasting effect. "Children are subject to many influences outside their homes, but parents have the most lasting influence".
        —Ray J. Maloney, Director, Self-Esteem Center
        Birmingham, Michigan

17. You build your child's self-esteem and your family-connectedness. "Every night tuck your child in bed and say something like 'we are so proud of you, we are so pleased with you, you are making us so happy, we are so grateful you are in our life,' and share specific things . . . 'you are such a great baseball player, you help out with the dishes, you are doing so well in school, you make us happy' and really let them know they are contributing and

they are doing fine and can relax and they don't need to worry so much."
—Jack Canfield, Motivational Speaker
Author, *Self-esteem and Peak Performance* (tape)

18. You form the world. "The little world of childhood with its familiar surroundings is a model of the greater world. The more intensely the family has stamped its character upon the child, the more it will tend to feel and see its earlier miniature world again in the bigger world of adult life. Naturally, this is not a conscious, intellectual process."
—Dr. Carl Gustav Jung (1875–1961)
Swiss Psychologist, Psychiatrist
"Father of Analytical Psychology"

19. You shape the future. "If you are a parent, recognize that it is the most important calling and rewarding challenge you have. What you do every day, what you say and how you act, will do more to shape the future of America than any other factor.

As mothers, we must value children enough to discipline them, spend time with them, be decent role models for them and fight for what they need from our communities and nation."
—Marian Wright Edelman
Founder, Children's Defense Fund

20. You love your child. The most "crucial area for making a better world is for parents to rear their children with love and understanding, teaching them by their own example the ideals of helpfulness, kindliness, and service to others."
—Dr. Benjamin Spock, Child-Raising Expert
Author of *A Better World for Our Children: Rebuilding American Family Values*

Traits of a hero

We are entering a time when our youth are openly saying they admire their parents, professionals are continuing to proclaim the importance of active parents, and finally parents are proudly returning to the concept that yes, committed parenting is an honorable responsibility. We are seeing signs that the government, schools, and even businesses are asking the question, "Who cares about kids?" and acknowledging that it is everyone's responsibility. It is both an individual and collective task, but you remain the main figure in this drama and I want you to get the credit for being the hero.

One of the most significant traits of heroic parents is that they give their children something called unconditional love—love in the form of caring at all times; appreciating your child's good deeds and behavior and also disciplining inappropriate behavior; admiring your child's uniqueness; providing guidance and support in your child's endeavors; and being devoted to the overall health and well-being of your child without stifling his need for individual growth. Essentially, unconditional love means loving your child in a manner that displays your ongoing interest and concern for the child. And it is giving in an ongoing way without expecting anything in return, not even a thank you.

Being a heroic parent requires a tremendous amount of energy, courage, and dedication. In the following story two parents are faced with a challenge that demands stamina and commitment, the kind only heroic parents can give.

Lynn and Tom worked hard for what they possess—a house, a motorboat, and a small business that is doing well. They thoroughly enjoyed the times they shared as their four sons grew up, including the many camping and boating trips. Over time all the sons moved out of their house and started lives of their own, except for Greg. Twenty-five-year-old Greg lives at home with his parents. His parents give him the care he needs now and has needed for the past six years. Greg is paralyzed from a construction accident that took place when he was 19 years old. While working as a roofer, he lost his balance and fell from the roof of a two-story house.

Greg was in a coma for over four months. Obviously his parents were devastated and shocked. Although the diagnosis for Greg's recovery was bleak, Tom and Lynn spent the majority of their days at his bedside, hoping and praying for his complete recuperation. It appeared to be a hopeless situation. But after four months of verbal stimulation from his family, daily exercises of his limbs by the medical staff, and an ongoing belief in recovery by friends and family, Greg responded to his mother and father with slight hand squeezes and eye movements. What followed were months and months of weekly tests, seemingly unending physical therapy, and ongoing assistance with life's daily functions of providing nourishment and daily hygiene for Greg.

His parents still continue to dedicate all of their resources to the improvement of Greg's health. This commitment includes the payment of innumerable medical bills from their savings, a great deal of time off from work and social activities, and a seemingly unlimited amount of energy and faith—essentially the giving of an unconditional love.

At a time in Tom's and Lynn's lives when all their sons should be "grown up" and the parents' commitment and support should be decreasing, an uncertainty such as this arises. A parent cannot feel or believe that their responsibility is ever over. Your children need your unconditional love today and always—in varying forms and amounts, yes, but in any case, that ongoing need for a strong relationship is there. If you will not be there for them, who will? Greg realizes the special aspect of their parent/child relationship that his parents have given him, as a child and now as an adult.

In Greg's eyes, his parents are heroes to the maximum—for truly his life depends on it.

I would like to remind you again that you are your child's number one hero and role model. I would also like to clarify how a child may see you as a hero. Essentially there are two causes for admiration. The first is an act or series of deeds, while the second is a commendable trait or characteristic of the parent. For some families admiration by a child is one or the other, in other families, both, and still others, none.

In my case, after experiencing what parenting is all about, I feel both my parents performed exceptional acts and have extraordinary traits but I would say my mother exemplifies more exceptional acts and my father exemplifies more extraordinary traits.

In 1956, my parents made the decision to travel to the United States from Germany. My mother and father had the courage to leave Germany during a time of unrest, unsure of what would be in store for our family in the United States. They left East Germany with just a few items that a family would take along on a day outing. Whenever my mother shares recollections of her life in Germany and our family's new life in the United States, I think of my mother as a hero. In Germany she was a school teacher, which I admire because it represents a strong commitment to developing our youth. Besides working with young children, she had five of her own, and also lost a sixth due to a miscarriage. And my mother gives her all in everything she does—full-time employee, mother, and now as a grandmother of seven. I am proud of her and so are my brothers and sister.

It wasn't until her sixty-fifth birthday that we finally recognized my mother for all she has done for us. We had a special party and invited family and close friends. As a gift we gave her a weekend at one of her favorite resorts, the Mohonk Mountain House in the Shawangunk Mountains, and also presented her with a framed expression of thanks. It read:

All Our Love

On your special day, we want to express our appreciation. We think back to our childhoods and the many things you did to take care of us, to make us happy, to help us grow.

As we look back from our perspective of things, you have devoted much of your younger life in raising all five of us and even now, in adulthood. So, from us to you and on all our behalf, we want to say thank you and we love you for giving us life, for taking care of us and for loving us.

Happy Birthday and Many More!

Love,   Your Four Sons and Daughter, June, 20, 1992

A hero is not always good in all areas of child-rearing and children do not necessarily see one or both parents as heroes. Barbara Bush in her autobiography, *Barbara Bush: A Memoir*, describes her childhood and says that she and her mother were never close—the two simply had bad chemistry: "It was unhappiness for both of us. . . . My father was my hero."

A hero is in the eyes of the beholder and my father is a perfect example. Although the five of us agree on the specialness of Mom, we have differing views on Dad. I think of my father as a hero in a number of ways. He not only participated in and survived World War II, he aided many men in need of medical attention while in the service. He was good in his profession, owning and operating a pharmacy in Germany. Yet he left a comfortable lifestyle in Germany to gain freedom for our family, and he worked many odd jobs here in the United States to support our family. But most impressive to me was the inner strength he displayed to me one day shortly before his death.

Even though that day was my birthday, my schedule was the same as it had been for the last month. My anticipated routine started with the normal one-hour drive to work, followed by a full day at the office followed by the one-hour drive to the hospital, at least an hour visit with my father, another half hour drive home, capped off by a late evening meal. As I left work that day, I thought about not visiting my father that night, because it was my birthday. I was tired and really looked forward to being with my family that evening. Yet something within me told me I should at least make a quick stop at the hospital, so I did.

I went into the room. It was completely dark. The lights were out and the curtains closed. As I quietly headed for the chair to sit and wait until my father woke, my father began to sing the entire "Happy Birthday" song to me and bestowed two helium-filled balloons on me. I was shocked and overwhelmed. My father had not sung "Happy Birthday" to me in over twenty years. He was present at all my celebrations but was rarely an active participant. He always let my mother buy the gifts and make the preparations, and he let the other people sing. But here he was in the hospital, with one leg amputated due to gangrene and the other leg also soon to be taken off, singing to me on my birthday. What a trooper! To be in such a weakened situation and yet have the inner strength to change his ways of twenty years and reach out in this way to me was a heroic action for him.

His health deteriorated quite rapidly after that, and he lost his other leg. He was determined though. Dad had one last goal left to accomplish. His desire was not to die in a hospital. When he got to the point that he weighed less than 90 pounds, was not eating, and was barely taking in any fluids, the hospital administration notified us that my father could no longer stay and suggested we put him in a long-term care facility.

My sister, a nurse, offered to set up a room for him in her house. On the morning of May 27, he was released from the hospital and, by afternoon, was made as comfortable as possible at my sister's house. By the next morning my father had died in his sleep, a man who achieved his last goal with courage and determination. A hero? In my eyes, yes.

It should be clear now that you are your child's number one hero. There are other heroes and role models in your child's life and that's good (we'll discuss this further in later chapters), but just remember the real hero is you as a parent— someone who cares about your child on a daily basis. You want the best for your children and they know it and appreciate it, maybe not in an outward way, but within themselves. If you are lucky their gratitude may someday surface. You are performing a deed that results in a significant positive change. A hero? Yes, absolutely. Today's family experts are saying this and our youth are validating it. You are a hero. Realize it, believe it. This is quite the title; I know it is well deserved. Enjoy this status and read on to explore how you can be the best hero, the light and the fire, in your child's life.

Parents are the number one role model in America today—hands down.

> *—Frank Failey, President,*
> *American Psychological Association*

2
Know and Share Your Values

The school will teach children how to read, but the environment of the home must teach them what to read. The school can teach them how to think, but the home must teach them what to believe.
  —*Charles A. Wells*
    Edythe Draper's Book of Quotations

Values. The term is almost as nebulous as *heroes* but much more important to the development and well-being of our children. Values include one's beliefs, ethics, and code of conduct. Values are what guide our thinking and actions. Values are vital to how your child will live his or her life and eventually how his or her family—your grandchildren—will be raised. Values show concern for others and help keep society safe and productive.

Many of the national hero recognition programs honor individuals who exemplify a certain characteristic or value. *The Reader's Digest* "Heroes for Today" magazine series identifies people who demonstrate courage, kindness, or decency. The Positive Thinking Foundation's America's Awards honors unsung heroes who personify the American character and spirit. Recent recipients of this award were recognized for exhibiting values such as trust, initiative, caring, charity, courage, and perseverance.

These programs single out a certain trait or attitude and provide us with wonderful examples of positive values. Parents as heroes, however, have a much more difficult distinction to uphold. Parents have the complex and long-term job of teaching the full gamut of life values. What we parents say, and particularly what we do each and every day, sets in motion the maturation process of values in our child. Your child's life conduct is determined by his or her personal values. Values regulate, discipline, and shape your child's life, as well as his or her relations with others. Values build inner character and outer personality. Values are the foundation for how your child acts and what your child does. And you are the major contributor for developing their values. What you believe, how you display these values, and the amount of support you give your child in developing positive characteristics contributes to establishing your child's values.

Many parents are looking to childcare centers and schools to assist with this task. This request is answered by various values education programs. Allen Traditional Academy supports a values education program in all 47 public schools in Dayton, Ohio. Bravery and trustworthiness will be among several lessons emphasized in the new school year. The Vision Pursuit Team promotes values education on the Menominee Indian Reservation in northeastern Wisconsin. And in Howard County, Maryland, a recently school board-formed committee is advancing a list of 18 values.

It is exciting to see these and other programs active in schools and communities, but the job of teaching values belongs in the home. Most human service professionals agree, but again, our youth also believe strongly in this concept. In a recent study, 80% (over 100,000 of the teens surveyed) said, "Values should be taught at home." Only 1% of these 126,000 teens thought TV, music or movies should be where kids learn most of their values.[1] What a wonderful proclamation by our youth!

We are fully aware that "actions speak louder than words." That is, setting an example is much more powerful than preaching to your child. The problem is many of today's parents are confused over what their own values are or they find it difficult to follow through on their beliefs, and our children are left perplexed. Our youth hear parents talking about the importance of values such as honesty, kindness, and commitment, yet are not seeing these values displayed. There is real confusion over what parents should believe, what they do believe, and what they are conveying to their children.

Realizing your values

We are now ready to examine the second major insight I want to share with you. The first insight discussed in chapter one was: Understand who your child's #1 hero and role model is—YOU!

The second of the five insights deals with you being the teacher of values at home. This is a two-step process.

Know and share your values— demonstrate them to your child

In the 1970's the term values clarification came to be because there was great concern that children were having difficulty understanding and displaying their values. *Values Clarification: A Handbook of Practical Strategies for Teachers and Students* is just one of the numerous books covering this topic introduced in 1972. This book offered 79 different activities to help uncover beliefs and attitudes. One of the most interesting strategies was entitled "Alligator River." The following story is considered the "X" rated version and gets you thinking about your values. As you read this story, rank the five characters from the most offensive character to the least objectionable.

Once upon a time there was a woman named Abigail who was in love with a man named Gregory. Gregory lived on the shore of a river. Abigail lived on the opposite shore of the river. The river which separated the two lovers was teeming with man-eating alligators. Abigail wanted to cross the river to be with Gregory. Unfortunately, the bridge had been washed out. So she went to ask Sinbad, a river boat captain, to take her across. He said he would be glad to if she would consent to go to bed with him preceding the voyage. She promptly refused and went to a friend named Ivan to explain her plight. Ivan did not want to be involved at all in the situation. Abigail felt her only alternative was to accept Sinbad's terms. Sinbad fulfilled his promise to Abigail and delivered her into the arms of Gregory. When she told Gregory about her amorous escapade in order to cross the river, Gregory cast her aside with disdain. Heartsick and dejected, Abigail turned to Slug with her tale of woe. Slug, feeling compassion for Abigail, sought out Gregory and beat him brutally. Abigail was overjoyed at the sight of Gregory getting his due. As the sun sets on the horizon, we hear Abigail laughing at Gregory.[2]

From this story above, can you begin to think of some values that are meaningful in your life? Write them down.

Values important to me:

_____

_____

_____

_____

_____

_____

_____

Many books continue to express the need for instilling and expressing positive values. While sharing a few of the ones I feel are most helpful for outlining positive values, I want you to continue to think which values are important to you. Be honest with yourself and realize which ones are the most significant in your life.

One of the most comprehensive books on the subject of values is filled with stories portraying values and introduces children to positive traits. *The Book of Virtues* by William J. Bennett focuses on ten virtues: Self-Discipline, Compassion, Responsibility, Friendship, Work, Courage, Perseverance, Honesty, Loyalty, and Faith.

Bennett offers brief introductions to each of these virtues and then offers many stories relating to each—filling over 800 pages in all! The book is a wealth of history, inspiration, and educational vignettes providing insights for you and your child. Here are brief descriptions of these virtues.

- Bennett describes *self-discipline* as one's own teacher, trainer, coach, and "disciplinarian."
- *Compassion* is a virtue that takes seriously the reality of other persons, their inner lives, their emotions, as well as their external circumstances.
- *Responsible* persons are mature people who have taken charge of themselves and their conduct, who own their actions, and own up to them—who answer for them.
- *Friendship* usually rises out of mutual interests and common aims, and these pursuits are strengthened by the benevolent impulses that sooner or later grow.
- *Work* is applied effort; it is whatever we put ourselves into, whatever we expend our energy on for the sake of accomplishing or achieving something.
- *Courage* is a settled disposition to feel appropriate degrees of fear and confidence in challenging situations.
- *Perseverance* is "hanging in there" when experiencing hardship or difficulty; it is crucial for anyone intent on doing good in the world.
- To be *honest* is to be real, genuine, authentic and bona fide.
- *Loyalty* marks a kind of constancy or steadfastness in our attachments to those other persons, groups, institutions, or ideals with which we have deliberately decided to associate ourselves.
- *Faith* is a source of discipline and power and meaning in the lives of the faithful of any major religious creed.[3]

Which of these qualities are important to you? Which of

these would your child say is displayed in your home? Which of these traits need further development in your home and with your child?

Authors Linda and Richard Eyre offer a variety of methods for teaching values to preschoolers, elementary age youth, and adolescents in their book *Teaching Your Children Values*. Two of their major points support what I have been saying: Values are best taught in the home and parents are the crucial exemplars and instructors. They concentrate on twelve values, six "values of being" and six "values of giving." The values of being are honesty, courage, peace, ability, self-reliance and potential, self-discipline and moderation, and fidelity and chastity. The values of giving are loyalty and dependability, respect, love, unselfishness and sensitivity, kindness and friendliness, and justice and mercy. Again take a moment to evaluate which of these are important in your life and which are you teaching your child.

The Eyres also share the why of teaching moral values to children. Besides citing that values are what makes our society safe and workable and that morality and value-oriented behavior help a child develop a sense of autonomy, independence, and confidence, they say "because teaching values is the most significant and effective thing we can do for their happiness."

Not only are individuals looking at values, organizations are offering resources related to values too. The Way To Happiness Foundation was organized specifically for individuals and organizations that want to distribute a booklet called *The Way to Happiness*. The booklet is described as "A Common Sense Guide to Better Living" and is a literary attempt to fight "the causes of crime, youth violence, and social decay." The 21 steps outlined in the booklet are:

1. Take care of yourself.
2. Be temperate.
3. Don't be promiscuous.
4. Love and help children.
5. Honor and help your parents.

6. Set a good example.
7. Seek to live with the truth.
8. Do not murder.
9. Don't do anything illegal.
10. Support a government designed and run for all the people.
11. Do not harm a person of good will.
12. Safeguard and improve your environment.
13. Do not steal.
14. Be worthy of trust.
15. Fulfill your obligations.
16. Be industrious.
17. Be competent.
18. Respect the religious beliefs of others.
19. Try not to do things to others that you would not like them to do to you.
20. Try to treat others as you would want them to treat you.
21. Flourish and prosper.[4]

Another organization, The Peale Center For Christian Living, offers guidance in the area of values with its booklet *Seven Values To Live By*. A value is defined as "a principle that reflects an ideal moral standard by which individuals guide their thoughts and actions, and from which society as a whole ultimately benefits." The seven values described in the booklet are: integrity, courage, enthusiasm, happiness, faith, hope, and love.[5] They are characterized in this way:

- Integrity is a firm adherence to a code of moral values.
- Courage is the strength to do what is right regardless of the consequences.
- Enthusiasm is a passion for life.
- Happiness is the state of well-being and contentment.
- Faith is the belief and trust in God.
- Hope is the expectation of success.
- Love is the selfless concern for all others.[6]

Obviously one's religious beliefs have a forceful impact on

the formation of values. How one demonstrates a commitment to a Higher Power and how one views and follows religious doctrines greatly affects how teenagers think and behave. How is your school, church, mosque, or synagogue teaching values? Do you find yourself following these programs? Are these programs supporting your beliefs and teachings?

One of the earliest books of virtues is, of course, the Bible. In Galatians 5:22-23, nine virtues are mentioned—love, joy, peace, patience, kindness, goodness, faithfulness, gentleness, and self-control. It is also interesting to note that the Bible also mentions vices such as neglecting God and others. The list is quite extensive and includes impure thoughts, lust, hatred, fighting, jealousy, anger, trying to be first, complaining, criticizing, thinking you're always right, envy, murder, idolatry, spiritism, drunkenness, wild parties, cheating, adultery, greed, stealing, and lying. (Galatians 5, Ephesians 5, 1 Corinthians 6, and Revelation 22)[7]

Certain churches are taking an active role in promoting the values in the Bible and the prevention of premarital sex with the "True Love Waits" campaign. Southern Baptists along with support from such diverse religious groups as the National Federation for Catholic Youth Ministry, the Pentecostal Church of God, and the Wesleyan church are promoting this program. The pledge of abstinence until marriage is outlined in a covenant card which reads:

> "Believing that true love waits, I make a commitment to God, myself, my family, those I date, my future mate, and my future children to be sexually pure until the day I enter a covenant marriage relationship."[8]

Because much of today's concern on values centers on teenagers engaging in sexual relations, it is worthwhile looking at what Search Institute is doing. Search Institute, located in Minneapolis, Minnesota, is dedicated to promoting the well-being of children and adolescents through scientific research, evaluation, consultation, and the development of practical resources. One of these resources is *Human Sexuality: Values and*

Choices, a fifteen-session curriculum written for seventh and eighth grade students and their parents. This curriculum was developed through a collaborative effort between Search Institute and HealthStart of St. Paul.

As part of six goals, *Human Sexuality: Values and Choices* strives to decrease the behavioral intention of students to engage in sexual intercourse. The seven values used in this course are equality, self-control, promise-keeping, responsibility, respect, honesty, social justice. These values are the foundation of its Values and Choices program. As part of the behavioral intention analysis, the Search Institute tested the strength of various influences on a student's intention to engage in intercourse as a teenager. Peer pressure does have some bearing on a student's belief that he or she is or is not likely to engage in sexual intercourse while a teenager. Their data shows that students who believe that having sex would please their boyfriend or girlfriend are also likely to predict they will have sex as a teenager (and the reverse is also true: students whose friends aren't urging sex are likely to say they will not have sex as teenagers). To no one's surprise, the research found that peer pressure is influential.

But the single greatest influence on the intention to engage in intercourse, significantly greater than the influence of their friends' opinions, was whether the student felt that "It is against my values for me to have sex while I am a teenager."[9]

Values are extremely important and powerful in what a child does and why. But before we concentrate too much on our children's values and actions, it is necessary to take a step back and take a final inventory of not only your values (beliefs and attitudes) but what you value.

Looking at what you value means examining your priorities, goals, and interests. An easy and true way to assess what you value is looking at what you spend your money on; how you use your time; how you treat other people and what type of relationships you have; and the way you complete a task or job. These four areas pretty much sum up what you value and how your values are projected.

Thomas J. Leonard, founder of Coach University, created an awareness activity called Tru Values Program. This exercise involves reading through a list of more than 150 values and initially selecting the 10 that resonate as values to you. You then narrow this list down to four values, with a value "being a MUST for you to be yourself." Although many of the items on Leonard's list are not what we think of as traditional values, this exercise is helpful. The Tru Values list represents your priorities, interests, and short descriptions of activities and experiences that you are attracted to and find excitement in. It involves, as Leonard would say, "telling the truth about what you actually value or love to do with your time."Take a few minutes to read this list and select 10 of these "new" values.

Values List

Adventure: risk, danger, gamble, experiment, the unknown, speculation, endeavor, exhilaration, thrill, dare, quest, venture.

Beauty: grace, attractiveness, magnificence, refinement, loveliness, gloriousness, elegance, radiance, taste.

To Catalyze: impact, turn on, spark, stimulate, move forward, unstick others, encourage, energize, touch, coach, influence, alter.

To Contribute: serve, assist, facilitate, provide, improve, endow, minister to foster, augment, strengthen, grant, assist.

To Create: design, imagination, conceive, perfect, invent, ingenuity, plan, assemble, synthesize, originality, build, inspire.

To Discover: learn, locate, discern, detect, realize, distinguish, perceive, uncover, observe.

To Feel: emote, to glow, energy flow, to experience, to feel good, in touch with, sense, be with, sensations.

To Lead: guide, cause, reign, persuade, inspire, arouse, govern, encourage, influence, enroll, rule, model.

Mastery: expert, dominate field, preeminence, outdo, dominate field, superiority, greatest, set standards, adept primacy, best, excellence.

Pleasure: have fun, sensual, be entertained, be hedonistic, bliss, play games, sex, be amused, sports.

To Relate: be connected, to unite, be bonded, part of community, to nurture, be integrated, family, be linked, be with.

Be Sensitive: tenderness, be present, show compassion, touch, empathize, respond, perceive, support, see.

Be Spiritual: be aware, related with God, honoring, be accepting, devoting, be passionate, be awake, holy, religious.

To Teach: educate, inform, prime, instruct, prepare, uplift, enlighten, edify, explain.

To Win: prevail, score, triumph, accomplish, acquire, predominate, attain, win over, attract.[10]

The Institute in Basic Life Principles, based in Oak Brook, Illinois, classifies the development of values as character training development. Character training is listening to your conscience and cooperating with it when it tells you what is right and what is wrong.[11]

Character training is more important than achievement. The Institute outlines 49 character qualities in their booklet *Character and Destiny.*

They list these qualities and also the corresponding negative character qualities. They are:

Alertness vs. Unawareness
Attentiveness vs. Unconcern
Availability vs. Self-Centeredness
Boldness vs. Fearfulness
Cautiousness vs. Rashness
Compassion vs. Indifference
Contentment vs. Covetousness
Creativity vs. Underachievement
Decisiveness vs. Double-Mindedness
Deference vs. Rudeness
Dependability vs. Inconsistency
Determination vs. Faintheartedness
Diligence vs. Slothfulness
Discernment vs. Judgment
Discretion vs. Simplemindedness
Endurance vs. Giving Up
Enthusiasm vs. Apathy
Faith vs. Presumption
Flexibility vs. Resistance
Forgiveness vs. Rejection
Generosity vs. Stinginess
Gentleness vs. Unthankfulness
Hospitality vs. Loneliness
Humility vs. Pride
Initiative vs. Unresponsiveness
Joyfulness vs. Self-pity
Justice vs. Fairness
Love vs. Selfishness
Loyalty vs. Unfaithfulness
Meekness vs. Anger
Obedience vs. Willfulness
Orderliness vs. Disorganization
Patience vs. Restlessness
Persuasiveness vs. Contentiousness
Punctuality vs. Tardiness
Resourcefulness vs. Wastefulness
Responsibility vs. Unreliability
Reverence vs. Disrespect

Security vs. Anxiety
Self-Control vs. Self-Indulgence
Sensitivity vs. Callousness
Sincerity vs. Hypocrisy
Thoroughness vs. Incompetence
Thriftiness vs. Extravagance
Tolerance vs. Prejudice
Truthfulness vs. Deception
Virtue vs. Impurity
Wisdom vs. Natural Inclinations[12]

One of the most extensive works on values is Professor Milton Rokeach's Value Survey from his book *The Nature of Human Values*. The survey explores terminal values and instrumental values. Rokeach describes terminal values as those representing end-state of existence, or what we might call accomplishments. The instrumental values are those representing mode-of-conduct or characteristics or traits. We can think of terminal values in terms of a child looking up to a hero for what the hero has accomplished. The instrumental values are specific characteristics which are admirable.

I hope you have been seriously thinking about your values because now I want you to rank your values using the Rokeach's Value Survey. Rank each set from one to 18, with one being the most important to you.

Terminal Values

____ A Comfortable Life—a prosperous life
____ Equality—brotherhood and equal opportunity for all
____ Exciting Life—a stimulating, active life
____ Family Security—taking care of loved ones
____ Freedom—independence and free choice
____ Health—physical and mental well-being
____ Inner Harmony—freedom from inner conflict
____ Mature Love—sexual and spiritual intimacy
____ National Security—protection from attack
____ Pleasure—an enjoyable, leisurely life
____ Salvation—saved; eternal life

____ Self-Respect—self-esteem
____ Sense of Accomplishment—a lasting contribution
____ Social Recognition—respect and admiration
____ True Friendship—close companionship
____ Wisdom—a mature understanding of life
____ World at Peace—a world free of war and conflict
____ World of Beauty—beauty of nature and the arts

Instrumental Values—Mode of Conduct

____ Ambitious—hardworking and aspiring
____ Broad-minded—open-minded
____ Capable—competent;effective
____ Clean—neat and tidy
____ Courageous—standing up for your beliefs
____ Forgiving—willing to pardon others
____ Helpful—working for the welfare of others
____ Honest—sincere and truthful
____ Imaginative—daring and creative
____ Independent—self-reliant; self-sufficient
____ Intellectual—intelligent and reflective
____ Logical—consistent; rational
____ Loving—affectionate and tender
____ Loyal—faithful to friends or the group
____ Obedient—dutiful; respectful
____ Polite—courteous and well-mannered
____ Responsible—dependable and reliable
____ Self-controlled—restrained; self-disciplined[13]

What are the values that are most important to you? Are they what you thought they would be? Are they the ones you are demonstrating at home? Are they the ones you want your child to learn?

Examining the values in your life is a pretty intense and thought-provoking exercise. I think there is one value that should be the central theme or focus in all that you and your child do. Think back to the values clarification exercise at the beginning of this chapter. What was the major value or moral that was missing? It took me many years to pinpoint exactly what the problem is with each of the characters. For me it was the lack of respect—the lack of respect for oneself and for others. Respect is the foundation and the umbrella that guide a true hero in what he or she does.

My wife, Sue, and I strive to instill respect in our two sons. For us respect means consideration, honor, regard, love, esteem, and kindness. If you look at what respect is, it is a unique combination of many values, particularly courage, love, honesty, and commitment. Respect relates to the many different facets of life: respect for others—adults and peers; a Higher Power; weather—wind, rain, and the sun; nature, including animals and water; fire; different people and cultures; life; health and sickness; the law; truth; guns; drugs; a job well done; and of course, respect for oneself—self-esteem.

In our house, this respect takes form in everyday activities and experiences such as returning a found baseball bat to the park director; apologizing for a harsh word said to a sibling; being kind to small children and the elderly who visit; saying "please" and "thank you" to family members; shaking hands with the opposing team members after a soccer or baseball game; completing homework assignments on time; picking up garbage along the roadside in our neighborhood; taking swimming lessons; extinguishing fires at the campground where we stay during the summer; and performing personal hygiene.

Values are taught in an ongoing way ranging from a notable event such as our son Ryan returning a bracelet found in our supermarket to the seemingly trivial act of not gossiping about neighbors or friends. All these daily activities, large or small, add to the foundation of your child's value system. As your child grows older, you have less and less control over his or her actions and you need to trust your child more and more. You have to believe you raised your child with a strong value system.

George and Mary found out about trusting themselves when it came to knowing their college-age daughter has a strong sense of respect for herself and others. When she wanted to go to Woodstock '94, George and Mary expressed their concern. They were not thrilled at her attending this event but they knew she was surely old enough to make such a decision. When talking with George and Mary, I found them quite calm over this episode and then I realized they believed that the values they had instilled during the last twenty years were going to provide the daughter with enough strength and wisdom to deal with any situation she might face at this event.

Today's concern for respect is not new to parents, in fact it has been a concern for over 2000 years. Socrates in 400 B.C. wrote: "Our youth now loves luxury. They have bad manners, contempt for authority, disrespect for older people. Children nowadays are tyrants . . . They contradict their parents, chatter before company, gobble their food, and tyrannize their teachers."

So how do we change this disrespectful behavior? It is probably best summed up from something almost as old, the Bible.

"And so you became a model . . ."(I Thessalonians 1:7)

Setting The Example

Every day we as parents are put in situations, big and small, that display our values, and this is keenly observed by our children. As you begin to evaluate your own values and the behavior you convey to those people around you, I would like to remind you on the importance of the example you are setting. The things you do and say are being absorbed by your child, right from an early age on up to adulthood. This poem is a reminder on the importance of what we say and do.

To Any Little Boy's (or Girl's) Father (or Mother)

There are little eyes upon you, and they're watching night and day,
There are little ears that quickly take in everything you say,
There are little hands all eager to do everything you do,
And a little boy who's dreaming of the day he'll be like you.

You're the little fellow's idol, you're the wisest of the wise,
In his little mind, about you no suspicions ever rise.
He believes in you devoutly, holds that all you say and do,
He will say and do in your way, when he's grown up, just
like you.

There's a wide-eyed little fellow who believes you're
always right,
And his ears are always open and he watches day and
night,
You are setting an example every day in all you do,
For the little boy who's waiting to grow up and be like
you.[14]
—Author Unknown

Teaching values is an ongoing process. It is necessary to
realize your own values and then instill them as early as possible. In H. Jackson Brown, Jr.'s book *Life's Little Instruction
Book*, Jackson Brown shares 511 suggestions, observations, and
reminders on how to live a happy and rewarding life. He wrote
the book for his son Adam. It includes advice that deals with
values including such advice as "Don't let your possessions
possess you" or "Observe the speed limit" or "Give your best
to your employer. It's one of the best investments you can
make." He gave the book to his son on his first day of college.
A few days after receiving the book, Adam called his father.
"Dad," he said, "I've been reading the instruction book and I
think it's one of the best gifts I've ever received. I'm going to
add to it and someday give it to my son."

After personally talking with Jackson Brown it become evident to me that this book was not intended to teach Adam values, just confirm them. Jackson Brown had already laid the
foundation of these values during his child's growing years so
Adam could be at this point now. Understand that imparting
family values is a long-term process. Start early. Then, during
the teens, reinforce the lessons.

I said it over and over again, "Use your left foot." I was
teaching Ryan the importance of using his left foot in soccer.

He tried a few times and reverted back to using his right foot. I felt discouraged. I knew what was right and that this would be vital toward him learning the proper and best way to play soccer. The next year I emphasized this point again, demonstrating it whenever possible and supporting his efforts when he did try it. This continued for a number of years, with him making slow progress each year, but leaving me with the feeling that "he just wasn't getting it."

But then it happened. A moment came in a game when, out of necessity, he had to use his left foot to kick a goal. He pulled his left foot back and solidly directed his foot at the ball and propelled it into the net. Ryan was ecstatic. He ran over to me and shouted, "I made a goal with my left foot. I even kicked it harder than with my right foot!"

I felt a surge of contentment rush through my body. Four years of explaining, demonstrating, and supporting his efforts had paid off. He exhibited what he had practiced and learned a lesson in this game.

Although kicking a ball is more of a skill than a value, the process is similar—first understanding what you want to teach your children, then demonstrating it by being the role model, and finally giving positive feedback when your child exhibits that behavior. It means telling them, showing them, and nurturing them many times over—a tedious but significant process of repetition, repetition, and repetition.

In a recent conversation I had with other fathers at work, our dialogue focused on the widespread drinking problem on college campuses. One of the men said his son told him that many of the students at his college drink, and drink excessively. The father went on to tell us how it hadn't been any better in the small town high school his son went to. The son had also told his father that most of the football team players drank whenever they could.

I began to think how acceptable drinking is in our society and how often television advertisements and movies make drinking so glamorous. Although the media is part of the problem, it goes back to family life and role models. It became clear that parents do not always offer positive examples, yet may still be seen as "heroes" and "role models" by their child. Values, whether good or bad, are learned by observation, imitation, and repetition. I flashed back in my mind to about twelve years ago when I was organizing weekend trips for fathers and their sons, known as Indian Guides, and fathers and their daughters, Indian Princesses. The boys and girls were between five and nine years old. The weekend trips were a favorite outing and good times were had by all—scrumptious food, fun games, and great fishing. There was one activity that bothered me—the excessive beer drinking by some fathers. I realized now why seeing these fathers drinking so much on the parent/child weekend troubled me so. All of these children are now grown up, and some of them may be the ones that are now plagued with drinking problems in high school and college because of the example set by their father.

My flashback was interrupted by another father recalling that a Westchester County high school soccer coach came to practice every Saturday drunk. These are the examples kids look up to, and then we wonder why the youth are involved in excessive drinking and smoking.

Oscar Greene, an inspirational writer, shares a more positive example of how his parents taught him by example.

His father and mother were domestics who cooked at college fraternity houses and in private homes. They worked from dawn to dusk, often seven days a week. During house parties their workday stretched into the morning hours without additional pay. When dishes and pots overflowed their employer's sinks, Oscar was expected to help.

His father and mother never complained. Their conversation echoed with love and admiration for their employers. But Oscar wanted no part of that kind of life. He was ashamed and felt employers took advantage of his father and mother. Why didn't they complain? Whey didn't they speak up for their rights?

He vowed to escape, but how? The answer: Get an education! So with scholarships, long hours in manual work and sacrifices at home, he completed college. From there, it was into teaching and on to industry. Ten years into industry and things boomed. He seized the opportunity and moved from the machine shop to engineering technician to senior technical writer. Education paid off and, secretly, he felt he had done it on his own.

Then, one day, his supervisor paused at his desk and said, "I would love to have met your parents. They taught you well. You are a worker and a gentleman."

He was stunned. So it wasn't his academic training that made the difference. His father and mother had received little appreciation, yet it was their devotion that had gained them the reputation for being skillful, industrious, honest, and diligent. By example, they had instilled all this in him. What a precious gift![15]

Three Major Aspects of Values

So what is the secret to becoming the best hero we can for our children when it comes to values? I would suggest we focus on three major aspects. The first is integrity. Denis Waitley, renowned motivator and author, says, "Integrity that strengthens an inner value system and sets an example for others is the real bottom line in every arena."

Dr. Nathaniel Branden, author, lecturer, and director of The Biocentric Institute in Los Angeles, states, "When your behavior expresses your professed values, you have integrity." It means wholeness, goodness, or honor. Integrity means feeling good about what you do, knowing it is the right thing to do, and being proud of your actions being copied. And what does "right" mean? It means you are not embarrassed, ashamed, or regretful for the action you take. A consultant with a high level of integrity suggests three quick tests to determine whether what you are doing is right. They are:

1. How does your stomach feel when talking or thinking about it?
2. How would you feel if whatever you're doing involved someone in your family?
3. How would you react if "60 Minutes" came to investigate what you are doing?

Integrity means having a certain built-in set of attitudes, according to author Arthur Gordon. Integrity means living up to the best in yourself. Integrity means having a highly developed sense of honor. Integrity means having a conscience and listening to it. Integrity means having the courage of your convictions. And integrity means obedience to the unenforceable, such as teaching and living positive values.[16]

Gordon suggests no sure way to acquire or teach integrity, but he does say that the first step is schooling yourself to practice total honesty in little things.

It is necessary to demonstrate truthfulness in your parenting role and this is, by no means, an easy task, as demonstrated in the following true story. The story shows how hard "living our values" can be, especially honesty.

The cold Iowa dawn was still an hour off, but already Dad and I had finished a big job on our farm. We had loaded 100 head of cattle for market into two waiting semi-trailers.

I was 16 and this was the first time I had seen the cattle taken to market. Dad had made it my job to keep the feeder full with the right mix. I had seen the cattle come in as scrawny yearlings and fatten up to 1,100 pounds apiece. The price was right and it was time to sell. There was just the paperwork to complete.

"Got to have your John Hancock right here," said Mick, one of the drivers, as he handed Dad a clipboard.

"What's this, Mick?" asked Dad.

"Something Uncle Sam wants you to sign. Says you kept your cattle off stilbestrol for two weeks before slaughter."

I felt the blood rush to my head. Stilbestrol was used as a feed additive to promote growth. We'd debated its use and had gone ahead. The government had changed its regulations several times, and the form Mick had was new. I'd been giving the cattle stilbestrol all along.

"I don't think it makes a whole lot of difference myself," said Mick. "Don't see how they can tell anyway."

Dad scratched the ground with his boot. We'd be the laughingstock of the county if we unloaded our cattle now because of some silly government regulation. Another two weeks and the market price would be sure to fall.

Finally Dad looked up. "Better unload 'em," he said.

That was 15 autumns ago and I'm a farmer myself now. Dad died a few years back. But his example lives on for me. That morning as the cattle came back down the chutes and daylight stretched across the horizon, Dad didn't say anything. He didn't have to. Honesty wasn't a value Dad talked about. It was something he lived by.[17]
—George H. Bierma, Sioux Center, Iowa

The second trait or aspect needed for parents as heroes relating to values is courage. Courage is humorously displayed in *The Wizard of Oz* but oh how difficult it is for the lion to have courage. As with honesty, in reality it is difficult to exhibit courage sporadically, but even more difficult to portray it in an ongoing way.

There's a story about Carl Erskine, former pitching great with the Brooklyn Dodgers who dominated baseball a generation ago, that helps us understand why we dedicate so much energy to pursuing this meaningful value, courage.

Erskine, now a bank president, spoke at a luncheon for corporate heads. The overall theme of the meeting was the importance of strong values in the drive to build and achieve. Those attending expected Erskine to give parallels between effort and achievement in baseball and success in business. They were wrong.

After a few enjoyable baseball anecdotes, Erskine said, "I have a couple of things I'd like to show you. First is this World Series ring," he said, sliding it off his finger. "I have two of these, and I always thought there could be nothing better than the feeling of winning a World Series and wearing the ring. I was wrong.

"This," he said, pulling a small plastic box from his pocket, "gave me a greater feeling. You see, this box contains the medal my disabled son Jimmy won swimming in the Special Olympics. For me, winning the World Series was a matter of sharpening and using God-given talents to their fullest potential. For Jimmy, this medal meant overcoming a desperate fear of water. It meant fighting against great odds to make muscles do things they were never able to do before. It meant standing up in front of a large and confusing crowd and getting from one end of the pool to the other without being distracted.

"So as we proceed to our goal of adding excellence to ability in order to achieve, let's not forget the most important values of love, courage, struggle, and perseverance against great odds."[18]

Although Carl Erskine may not admit it, he too set a wonderful example of courage, determination, and caring in all he did, as well as in respecting and supporting his child. Erskine and his wife Betty worked to form an organization that would help meet the special needs of children like their son. Through their own courage, struggle, and perseverance, the idea materialized into the Hopewell Center, which today operates with a two million dollar annual budget and provides a preschool, an infant stimulation program, a sheltered workshop, group homes, and job placement for children with multiple disabilities. And because of his courage and commitment during those difficult parenting years, Erskine reaped a reward bigger than any sports award or Hollywood recognition ceremony could

give out—seeing the strong inner character and outer personality of the child he helped to shape.

The third value is love. Sue and I make a concerted effort to
express our love in the form of hugs, kisses, and words of affection. It is a priority for me to express love regularly. I want my
sons to know they are loved. I even make it a point to hug and
kiss them before I go for my jogs on Saturdays and Sundays.
While Ryan was a toddler, I played a little game with him. I
would say, "You know what? I love you as big as—" and I completed the sentence with something big such as a bulldozer or
an office building. As Ryan grew the items grew also until we
got as "big as the world" and "as big as the universe."

Since Zachary reached the age of two, he and I have done
the same thing, but the game has changed just a little bit. I ask
Zachary, "You know what?" And we both reply as quick as
possible with "I love you. I miss you. You're terrific!" When I
say this phrase faster than him, I continue with "I win." And
Zachary astutely replies, "Nobody wins. You only win at
games."

Values are not skills nor games; rather they are a collective
way of believing and living. It is so important for your values
and actions to agree because there can be no happiness if the
things we believe in are different from the things we do. And a
corollary to this thought is that there can be no real happiness
if your values are destructive or disrespectful in nature for you
or others. If you help your child develop strong habits of being
kind to others, being honest, and having courage, your child
will have a solid foundation on which to build his or her own
personality, interests, and eventually his or her own family.

Again and again we come back to two basic concepts for
teaching values by a parent—the need of knowing what your
values are and then demonstrating the positive ones to your
child in an ongoing way. Realizing your values means looking
at the many values we discussed, then getting an accurate
measurement of which values you are displaying to your family, and finally becoming the example of these values for your
child.

After becoming aware of your values, the second step is

demonstrating the positive values. James H. Thom shares this thought, "If you try to improve one person by being a good example, you're improving two. If you try to improve someone without being a good example, you won't improve anybody."

And once you bring what you are doing in alignment with what you believe in, you will find contentment and happiness for yourself and raise a child with a well-established value and belief system.

> *The stages of the Noble Path are: Right View, Right Thought, Right Speech, Right Behavior, Right Livelihood, Right Effort, Right Mindfulness, and Right Concentration.*
> —*Buddha (B.C. 568-488)*

3

Strengthen Your Child's Self-esteem

Love your children with all your hearts, love them enough to discipline them before it is too late . . . Praise them for important things even if you have to stretch them a bit. Praise them a lot. They live on it like bread and butter, and they need it more than bread and butter.
>   —Lavina Christensen Fugal
>   Edythe Draper's Book of Quotations

Self-esteem. Self-esteem means confidence and satisfaction in yourself. It is an internal honoring of yourself. It is feeling satisfied in who you are and what you do. A high self-esteem gives you a sense of peace and harmony. It involves having integrity and respecting yourself and others. And self-esteem is directly linked to manifesting positive values and promoting good mental health.

Before working at Guideposts Associates, I was what I call a professional self-esteem builder for youth and adults. I organized recreational and educational programs and activities at the YMCA, camps, and a fitness club. I worked hard on creating activities and experiences that would build the self-esteem of participants. I was aware of the importance of children developing high self-esteem at an early age. But then in 1986, my eyes were opened even wider regarding the importance of high self-esteem. Ryan, our first child was born in February, and then a unique experience took place in the Catskill Mountains. . . .

My friend Mike and I were hiking in the middle of the

Catskill Mountains in upstate New York. We were deep in the woods. In fact, there were no trails. We bushwhacked, meaning we used map and compass and blazed our own trail from Fir Mountain to a peak known as Big Indian. All signs of civilization were gone including car sounds, houses, and to our delight, trash. We enjoyed the crisp, clean, autumn air and the beauty of the fall foliage as we walked. At one point, my eye caught something white like a large mushroom. I investigated and, to my surprise, discovered it was a piece of paper. How odd, a piece of garbage here, literally out in the middle of nowhere. I picked it up and read the writing.

This balloon was released from Latham Elementary School on May 9, 1986. Please write and let me know where you found my balloon. I'll write back to you.

It was signed Annette Reynolds (name changed), Grade 3.

I felt like I had just found a treasure. Imagine finding this note way out here. Surely this balloon must have traveled the farthest from Annette's school. I had to write Annette immediately. The next day I wrote to her in care of the school and received the following reply a few weeks later:

Dear Steffen or Mr. Kraehmer?
I am very, very sorry for taking so long. I hope you will forgive me. I don't know if my balloon traveled the farthest or not. I was deeply grateful for your letter. I am very busy. I am a bright child and hate it! I need someone to talk (write) to about how I feel, no one understands me. Everyone is always asking me for answers, sometimes how and/or why I master sports so easily. Sometimes I try to lower my grades by answering wrong. Everyone calls me names and says I think I'm a "hot shot" because I'm bright and (they don't know it but) very bored. What can I do? Please write back. I have enclosed a so-so picture of you, also one of me. I need a pen pal.
    Love,
    Miss Reynolds   (Annette)

P.P.S.S. 1. I think "Miss Reynolds" is a beautiful name. Call me either. 2. There's one thing I stink at: spelling.

I was shocked and saddened by the letter. Here was a bright and athletic child with low self-esteem.

This was upsetting enough, but more disturbing was the fact that here was a ten-year-old child reaching out to a complete stranger regarding her problems!

Dr. Nathaniel Branden, author and leading innovator in the "psychology of self-esteem," expresses the importance of good self-esteem in this way: "I cannot think of a single psychological problem from anxiety and depression, to fear of intimacy or of success, to alcohol or drug abuse, to underachievement at school or at work, to spouse battering or child molestation, to sexual dysfunctions or emotional immaturity, to suicide and crimes of violence, that is not traceable to the problem of poor self-esteem."[1]

Given the fact that low self-esteem has been implicated in a host of deleterious adolescent behaviors including delinquency, drug abuse, suicidal behavior, academic underachieving, and dishonesty, a recent study suggests parental support, acceptance, approval, and affirmation as vital antidotes to the pernicious side-effects of low self-esteem during adolescence. Strong, nurturing parent-adolescent relationships serve to buffer many of the negative effects of adolescent change, offering an arena of comfort in the midst of the adolescent sea of discontinuity.[2]

To be an inspirational hero to your child, keep focused on building your child's self-esteem. You must provide ongoing support, acceptance, approval, and affirmation. Building a child's healthy self-concept is vital.

A good self-image includes three major characteristics: A person with high self-esteem is a satisfied, confident, and responsible individual.

We as parents should work hard at building a child's self-esteem. The goal again is to raise a child who is satisfied ("I like myself"), confident ("I can do it"), and responsible ("I am responsible for my behavior").

Each child is different in personality, physical appearance and well-being, and interests. Children feel good about themselves when they are doing something they enjoy or when they are creating something. To help a child discover his or her talent, skill or gift the child should be in a variety of activities and receive positive feedback. Danny Thomas once said, "All of us are born for a reason, but all of us don't discover why." Keep watch for your child's favorite interests and support them. Satisfaction in an activity gives rise to increased confidence, and confidence renders personal values, which in turn contributes to building a responsible and emotionally healthy person. This confidence-building process is a cycle that begins with pleasurable experiences.

After the first day of school, Ryan rushed home, went into the garage, gathered the items he needed and began whittling. He loves to whittle. It is relaxing and provides him with a feeling of accomplishment. This hobby may just be a short-term interest but it is one that we are supporting as just one way to build his self-esteem. Although this may seem like an insignificant interest it does offer the three ingredients for improving his view of himself: Whittling gives Ryan satisfaction, builds his confidence, and develops a sense of responsibility, especially in regards to using a knife.

Your child's participation in an enjoyable hobby or activity may be short-lived or it may develop into a major pursuit. Shaen Marks, 11, from Sacramento, California, has been lacing up roller skates since he was four years old—and competing in national competitions since first grade. Brianne Schwantes, 13, from South Milwaukee, Wisconsin, went to Iowa to help with flood relief. Her dedicated volunteerism provided her with the opportunity to meet both President Bill Clinton and Pope John Paul II. Christopher Fyhr, 12, from Cranford, New Jersey visited the LEGO factory in Denmark, as a prize in a national LEGO-building contest when he was five years old. Lynsey Long, an 11-year-old ballerina, was one of the 50 Americans chosen to attend a six-week program in Vail, Colorado, with Madame Golovkina, director of the Moscow Academy. Twelve-year-old Sam Stern loves to bake and wins first-place ribbons for his efforts at the El Paso County Fair in Colorado. And Matt Whiteis, 9, remembers the day his dad bought him his first baseball card. He was two years old. Now his 5,000 card collection excites neighborhood friends and fellow classmates.

Having high self-esteem means your child feels worthy. Sam Levenson, a teacher, writer, and humorist, wrote this on the worth of each and every child: "There's an old Talmudic teaching which says that every child is born with a message to deliver to the human race, a few words, maybe a work of art, maybe a bench he'll build, maybe something he'll say that completes the explanation of why we're here." Positive and pleasurable experiences are key to finding satisfaction and confidence and a sense of purpose.

While participating in everyday activities, your child is not always experiencing positive feedback. Many times others tear him or her down. Those "others" can include teachers, coaches, peers, and yes, even you. Research done by the University of Iowa found that, on the average, a two-year-old child hears 432 negative statements in one day. In that same 24-hour period, that child hears only 32 positive statements. That is a ratio of almost 14 to 1, negative to positive![3] And this hindering ratio continues throughout the child's upbringing.

We need to create what I call an esteem bank. In the book *Marriage Insurance* author Willard F. Harley, Jr. talks about a Love Bank in a marriage. Harley says we are born with a Love Bank and every experience you have with people affects the balances in your account. When you associate a good feeling with a person, love units are deposited into the Love Bank. But bad feelings cause love units to be "withdrawn" from the account. This same concept can be used regarding building your child's esteem and confidence.

Our responsibility is to enhance our children's self-esteem in an ongoing way, to help our children be the best they can be. An esteem bank is built and enhanced by the following ten actions:

- Keep the critical comments about your child to a minimum and compliment your child in a sincere and ongoing manner.

- Help your child find acceptable ways of expressing himself/herself including the development of good language skills.
- Let your child make decisions.
- Foster your child's creativity and uniqueness.
- Delight in your child's accomplishments and victories including posting your child's work on the refrigerator or a bulletin board.
- Support your child's school work.
- Give your child freedom to explore and encourage your child to try new things.
- Answer your child's questions.
- Give your child the opportunity to be the teacher of an activity or a game, whether to other children or adults, including yourself.
- Listen in a non-judgmental manner to your child's hopes and dreams as well as his or her cares and concerns.

The above actions are ways you can build your child's self-esteem and help your child find his or her special gift. I've shared these with you, parent to parent. Now let me share with you some additional actions that a child outlines in this poem, child to parent:

Let me know when I make you proud. And help me to have pride in my own accomplishments.
Let me earn your trust. Then trust me.
   I won't let you down
Let me know you love me. With a hug. Or a pat on the back.
Or, when I need it, with a firm but gentle "no."
Let me be. Let me change. Let me grow.
Let me tell you when I'm feeling bad. Or angry. Even at you. And let me know that even on my worst days, you still like me.
Let me dream. Share my joy when my dreams come true. Share my tears when they don't.

Let me feel secure in my home. Help me realize that love is
   always there . . . that I can depend on you no matter what.
Let me run . . . let me laugh . . . let me play.
And most of all, let me be a child.
   Anonymous

Yes, your youngster is growing up, but he or she is still a
child and hopefully always will be. By being a child I mean
someone who is learning, growing, being open to new experiences, and finding ways to enjoy each and every day. It means
having the confidence to experiment, to try new things, to
understand it is okay if things do not turn out as you planned.

When I had the opportunity to take a series of classes to
learn the Microsoft Office software, I remember one morning
during a PowerPoint class feeling frustrated and confused. I
became increasingly flustered and annoyed. At lunch time, I
focused on why I wasn't learning and enjoying this class like I
did the other classes. I thought about how the three people
around me were involved and having fun with this class. I
wanted to do that, too. I realized I needed to be less concerned
with what others thought and about how many mistakes I was
making. My concern about what others thought was hindering
my learning and growing. I reminded myself what learning is
all about—experimenting, sometimes failing, and trying again.
That experience gave me renewed awareness of what it must
be like for my two sons in school, and I found a new appreciation for the position they find themselves in every day they go
to school. I was reminded of the importance of daily, positive
feedback, those deposits needed for a child's esteem bank. As
an adult we can give ourselves that needed boost, but for our
children we need to be parents as heroes.

I returned to the class with a new outlook, one that was like
a child—open to learning and receptive to experiencing new
tasks and ways to use a computer. I allowed myself, as it were,
to run . . . to laugh . . . to play . . . to be a child. This kind of outlook can make a tremendous difference in how we feel about
ourselves. It is vital in building both our own self-esteem and
our child's.

Of course, self-esteem is more than just having fun, it is being responsible for your actions and being considerate of others. The California Task Force to Promote Self-Esteem and Personal Social Responsibility defines self-esteem as "appreciating my own worth and importance and having the character to be accountable for myself and to act responsibly toward others."[4]

An analysis of the research and scholarly literature suggests a number of significant findings and generalizations about the importance and the effects of self-esteem upon youth and adults. Overall it would appear that self-esteem can be envisaged as a "social vaccine," a dimension of personality that empowers people and inoculates them against a wide spectrum of self-defeating and socially undesirable behavior.

Other compelling generalizations to be made include the following:

• The family is a strong force in the development of self-esteem. The early years are particularly important in establishing an "authentic and abiding self-esteem" in a person.

• High parental self-esteem is crucial to the ability to nurture high self-esteem and personal effectiveness in children.

• Writers and researchers show general, although by no means complete agreement, on the preconditions necessary for someone to demonstrate high self-esteem. Among the commonly used terms are: security, connectedness, uniqueness, assertiveness, competence, and spirituality.[5]

Brian Tracy, one of America's leading authorities on the development of human potential, describes the role of parenting this way. "The role of parenting is to nurture (your child's) high self-esteem."What a wonderful and positive way of looking at what we need to do as parents. But I think there's more than just a child's self-esteem. With this I will give you the third insight.

Strengthen your child's self-esteem and family-esteem

Before explaining the third insight in more detail, let's review what the two previous insights were:

1. Understand who your child's #1 hero and role model is—YOU!
2. Know and share your values—demonstrate them to your child.

In recent years a tremendous emphasis has been put on self-esteem as one of the primary causes for many of the serious problems in our contemporary society. This widespread concept is now being looked at as a possible myth. Some researchers (particularly Professor Wesley R. Burr and Clark Christensen) are now suggesting that by just concentrating on an individual's self-esteem we may be making some human problems worse and even creating new problems for the people we are trying to help. They suggest that as long as we continue to believe that it is an individual's self-esteem that is the key to human growth, development, health, and well-being, we will continue to create an environment that produces many people who are basically isolated, lonely, unconnected in deeply meaningful ways, and frustrated in trying to attain the richness that is possible for the human race.

Burr and Christensen believe the current emphasis on self-esteem and the content of most of the programs that have been developed to try to help people increase their self-esteem actually tend to promote such conditions as alienation rather than connectedness and bondedness, distance in human relationships rather than deep and enduring intimacy, superficial rather than in-depth relationships, temporary rather than enduring solutions, and an overemphasis on rational rather than emotional processes.[6]

Wow, what a revolutionary view! Or is it? How should we react to an extreme concept that building a child's self-esteem can be harmful and that more attention should be paid to building relationships? How about with an open mind! Let's stop for a moment and focus in on what I believe is a much more balanced and helpful definition of the role of parenting—one that takes into account these opposing views of self-esteem. The late Hodding Carter Jr., the Pulitzer Prize-winning editor of the Greenville, Mississippi, *Delta Democrat-Times* said it best, "There are two lasting bequests we can give our children. One is roots. The other is wings." To me this means developing self-esteem (wings) and also strong family relationships (roots).

The concentration on self-esteem recommended by Nathaniel Branden, Brian Tracy, and many other family practitioners fulfills the need for giving our children wings, but I feel strongly that there is a lack or void in giving our children the second bequest—roots—the support system family members need. Why? Perhaps it is because of busy two-career households, the increasing number of children being raised by a single parent, downsizing and economic hardships, confusion or lack of interest in our educational system, or the tremendous influence the media, particularly television and movies, has on our youth. All of these influences present major roadblocks as we try to raise our families successfully, that is, to give our children roots and wings.

I do think the majority of today's parents want successfully to raise a family and are trying hard. Parents realize the role of families as building blocks of society but are finding this task to be difficult, complex, and time-consuming. I recently saw a coffee mug by Shoestring Greetings that sums up the difficult task of parenting: "Raising children is like raising corn. It's hard work, it takes a lot of time, and there's no money in it!" How true!

But there is hope.

I've met and worked with many parents who are willing to dedicate their energies to raising their child properly. Their focus and actions emphasize creating a family that:

- shows care and concern to their child
- acknowledges the value of each family member
- has fun times together
- communicates in a positive, ongoing way
- has found a balance between being an individual and being part of a family

The actions these parents take are building family-esteem.

Family-esteem means having an active role in a support system. Family-esteem offers stability, a surrounding that provides unconditional love, growth, and sharing. Family-esteem fosters acceptance; the child knows that "My family loves me." Family-esteem implies being valued—"My family appreciates me." Family-esteem includes enjoyable times—"We (my family) have fun." It also means there is an understanding between family members—"My family communicates." And there is an equilibrium in the family. There is harmony in the home and in each individual's life. Each person believes "My family life is balanced."

For parents who are looking for this right blend of freedom and security for their family members, I want to share with you 30 ways to build family-esteem that honor each family member and the family as a whole. These are 30 practical ways to develop what I call family-esteem or essentially the roots for the family—roots that will provide family compassion, family strength, family vitality, and family character. And the exciting part about developing family-esteem is that it automatically contributes to the development of the child's self-esteem!

BUT for these methods to work requires more than just your involvement. It demands a commitment. Now you may be asking, Just what is the difference between involvement and commitment? Let me help you understand this major difference with this humorous metaphor.

Consider a breakfast consisting of bacon and eggs. The chicken was obviously involved in the preparation of the breakfast but the pig definitely made a commitment!

Before we proceed with outlining these 30 activities, I hope you will agree with these two ideas:
1. I want my child to become a lovable, capable, worthwhile, peak-performing individual and family member.
2. We, as parents, have the opportunity to play the most important role, a heroic role, in helping our children acquire skills and develop self-esteem.

I feel certain that if you have picked up this book you have already made the commitment to raise your family to the best of your ability. With this commitment, your unconditional love for your child(ren), and the suggestions in this book, I know you will raise a family that will give your child both the self-esteem (wings) and family-esteem (roots) they need and deserve.

Take time now to study the following inventory of 30 family-esteem builders. These, along with the 10 self-esteem builders mentioned earlier, should be used in an ongoing, consistent manner to build up and refill your child's esteem bank. Which ones are you using and which ones can you incorporate?

My family loves me

1. Seek Health for All Family Members. Obviously a major first in showing that you care about your child is making the child's physical well-being a priority. This tells the child you care a great deal about him or her. This care includes visits to the doctor and dentist, proper nutrition, and a consistent amount of exercise.

My wife Sue assists in the classrooms of our local school. She works with a first-grader who has difficulty seeing. Sue asked Mark if he wears glasses. Mark said "Yes, but they are broken." The parents were notified and did not feel it was a priority to replace his glasses. Mark is having a difficult time in the class and is becoming noticeably more introverted.

Your child needs to know you care about his or her health and that you also are caring about your own well-being.

2. Get Physical. Give your child hugs, "high-fives," and handshakes. An organization called Hugs Unlimited recommends the following daily prescription: 4 Hugs for survival; 8 Hugs for maintenance; and 12 Hugs for growth. Not a bad prescription for family-esteem, so hug your child and also dance, wrestle, give piggy-back rides, and roll or sleigh ride down hills with them. Touch is so necessary in fostering a relationship of love and caring.

3. Tell Them, Go Ahead. Tell your children that you love them. And tell them repeatedly. All too often in our relationships we take it for granted that our special person knows we love them.

A mother was unexpectedly called into work. She explained the situation to her daughters who were playing outside, saying, "You know I want to stay. I love you so much." The girls smiled and continued playing. The mother went to work.

Tell them. Go ahead. Let your children know you love them. It is as vital as caring for their health and giving them hugs.

4. Be an Athletic/Activity Supporter. Attend as many of your child's school, church, sports, and class functions as possible. A man shared with me that one of the most influential aspects of his growing up was that his father made it to every sports game or function he was in. Imagine that, EVERY ONE! You know this man's father is his top hero because of this.

5. Reach Out. There are some rough times for all families. When these times occur, whether because of financial, health, or communication problems, discuss this with your child and then ask for outside help. This can be through a United Way agency, your church or synagogue, or your neighbor. Your child will see this as a strength and a sign that you are reaching out for help because you care so much for the family.

Over 20,000 family members are reaching out through FIND, the Family Information Network Database, a national service I created for *Guideposts Magazine.* They ask for help and because of this, their family is finding assistance and growing stronger.

6. Pray with/for Your Child. There's power in prayer. National surveys show that 80% of Americans believe in the power of prayer—what an effectual way to build a family bond. For the annual *Guideposts* Magazine Family Day of Prayer, over 20,000 parents write asking for prayers for their family members.

Spend time worshiping together. Praying with your child or for your child definitely demonstrates love and appreciation for your child.

My family appreciates me

7. Work on Something Together. Do things together, not only vacation-type activities but nifty things like working on a puzzle, gardening, recycling, or household chores. Rearrange furniture in your home, have a garage sale, make a card and present for an ill friend or family member, or cut out pumpkins. These are good projects for all family members to have a contributing role. And don't forget to thank everyone for their contributions. You could also post the names of all who worked on it.

Our family bought a 125-pound pumpkin from a local farmer for $8.00. That alone was something to talk about, but the most exciting part was cutting this giant squash up and displaying it on Halloween. Each one of us played an influential role in preparing this pumpkin. And we received an unexpected note of appreciation by those who admired it on Halloween evening.

8. Get the Value Out of Meals. Eat at least one meal together. First, have everyone participate in some aspect of the meal preparation or clean-up. Then while eating, show an interest in your child's day and ask more than just yes and no questions. And again thank your children for their assistance. And once a month take the family out for dinner. Going out for dinner is the "appreciation bonus."

9. Clean Up Your Act! Want your family to take pride in your home and yard?Then organize an indoor clean-up detail and an outdoor seasonal task schedule. Everyone feels good after a job such as this is finished. Give out certificates to all workers involved. Today's computer programs are a wonderful tool for creating certificates of all kinds.

10. Think Safety. Have everyone participate in a first aid, water safety, or fire safety course. This not only shows your concern for your child but lets them know you need them and that their knowledge during an emergency is critical. Tell them that their interest and skills are appreciated in the area of safety.

11. Do "A Random Act of Kindness." Catch them doing something nice and let them know it. All too often we catch our children doing things wrong. In our local public school, as in most schools, the principal is the bad guy because when a child is sent down to see him, it means the child did something wrong. This school starting sending children down to him when they did something right.

And the "best" act of kindness: smile at your child. The smile is one of the most underrated actions that boosts a person's self-esteem. In a letter to *Psychology Today* magazine, Dr. Robert Healy wrote about a patient who had come to him for therapy after having changed his mind about committing suicide.

It seems that the young man had planned to jump off a bridge when something strange happened. While driving his car to the bridge, he stopped at a traffic light. Looking toward the sidewalk, he spotted an elderly woman who was smiling at him. He felt himself smiling back.

The light changed and he drove on, but the memory of her kindly face stayed with him.

Later, he told the psychologist, "Her smile made me think that perhaps I wasn't so bad after all."[7]

Never underestimate the power of your smile.

12. Write? Right! Many of the card companies have created a card for every occasion to give to your child. That is wonderful if you have the time to go to a card shop and want to spend a few dollars on each card. Instead get some index cards, small note pads or post-it notes and leave your child messages. And lots of them. Make them positive and especially sincere. After discussing this idea to parents at a seminar, a couple shared with me how this one act alone within only a week times resulted in a much more positive response from their teenager when it came to helping around the house. Believe me, it works.

My family has fun

13. Get Out! Enjoy the outdoors and nature. What a wonderful way to have a good time. Go for a walk. Go camping, whether at a campground or in your own back yard. And don't forget to roast marshmallows on the campfire! And if your camping trip results in a not so enjoyable experience at the time, it might still be remembered as a positive experience later on. Many times the worst experience out of doors still results in a strengthening of your family.

One of the most miserable camping times our family experienced was when we were out in a terrible thunderstorm at a New York State campground. But we look back on that time and laugh at how we huddled so close together in fear of the rain and lightning around us. It was frightening then and is funny now.

14. Get Reading. Go to the library. Read to your child and let your child read to you. Get some funny books, or magazines. Make your own book or journal. Fill it with favorite snap shots and put funny captions underneath. Take an idea from a book and put on a skit. Our family enjoys books in which we need to locate objects or people such as *Where's Waldo?*

The national school program PARP, Parents As Reading Partners, promotes reading and offers a wonderful reward for completing the program—a book. The Sibling Information Network Newsletter has a wonderful feature called "Reading is Fun." It lists interesting and humorous books for the whole family to enjoy.

15. Get Fit. Go for walks, jogs, bike rides, or ski trips. Make these outings into special events. A mother shared how the family loves to ski together. She said that the one time her daughter broke her leg—a seemingly negative event—has become the family's most fondly remembered ski trip.

16. Get Going . . . on Vacations. Get your family together to plan vacations. Make them fun ones. A father mentioned how each year his family relaxes at a beach for a whole week. The kids love the sand and water, and the parents love the quiet time. Make your vacations "true" vacations, that is, fun times for your whole family.

17. Get in the Picture. Take pictures and lots of them. Use them to create postcards or Christmas cards. You can find companies now that will make up personal calendars with a different family picture each month. These calendars can provide a daily reminder of fun times together. And keep those calendars and photo albums accessible for your child to look at. Participating in an event is obviously fun but so is remembering via pictures.

18. Get "Nosy." Take time to smell the roses. Lay on the grass and look at the clouds or stars at nighttime. Sit at the kitchen table and tell funny stories. Go outside and throw or kick a ball around. A mother of eight shared how every Saturday all eight children come into the parents bed for cuddling, wrestling, and having fun. What a wonderful way to enjoy each other.

My family communicates

19. Listen, Listen, Listen. A story by Richard C. Meyer points out the importance of listening.

"A sociologist on an African jungle expedition held up her camera to take pictures of the native children at play. Suddenly the youngsters began to yell in protest. Turning red the sociologist apologized to the Chief for her insensitivity and told him she had forgotten that certain tribes believe a person has lost one's soul if one's picture was taken. She explained to him, in detail, the operation of the camera. Several times the Chief tried to get a word in, but to no avail. Certain she had put all the Chief's fears to rest, the sociologist then allowed him to speak. Smiling, he said, 'The children were trying to tell that you forgot to take off the lens cap!' "[8]

Listen when your child is talking. It is essential.

20. Be Courteous in the Family Manner. Manners and politeness show you care and are aware of others around you. And "I'm sorry" is a major part of being courteous. Remember, you are setting the example.

Jennifer Birkmayer in *Discipline is Not a Dirty Word* offers this thought: "We all make mistakes. We all 'do the wrong thing' with our children. Lucky for us, most children are remarkably tough, loving and forgiving people. So if you goof, don't give up. But try again. And don't be afraid to say to your child, 'I'm trying to work out some ways of being a better parent. What I just did was not what I want to do. I'm sorry and I'm going to try again.'"[9]

21. Don't Make Derogatory Comments. Don't make negative comments. They hurt and they hurt a lot. Are they helpful in any way? I don't think so. Sidney B. Simon in his book *Negative Criticism* describes negative criticism as being like knives which people stick in us. He demonstrates how these critical jabs, sharp barbs, and deadly thrusts are not good for us, as our society somehow believes. It is not true that the more it hurts, the better it is for us. That is not the mark of being a grown-up woman or man.

I'm a firm believer in the saying "If you don't have anything nice to say, don't say anything." And this applies to all family members.

22. Keep Everyone Informed. Children, like adults, like to be informed. Tell them what's going on in your life and why. Whether it be a change in a job, moving, or the addition of a new family member, trust them with information and be there to support them if the news is bad.

A mother received devastating news. Her doctor informed her that she had breast cancer. She realized it would be necessary for the family to know this. Time was dedicated after an evening meal to inform the children. Initially the three children were shocked by the news. After this news sunk in, the family discussed how it would change their lives. This interaction and sharing brought a closeness to the family, a strength that is helping the family members cope and remain stable.

23. Shut Off the TV. How many more studies do we need to realize the television can be a major destroyer of family communication and closeness! Television stifles communication big time.

In the Muppet Kids book *TV or Not TV* Gonzo has a bad case of STATIC. STATIC stands for Somewhat Terribly Awful Television-Itis Condition. It means not paying attention to anyone, not doing homework, never going outside.

Enjoy television programs but limit viewing time.

24. Tell Her/Him about Adult Subjects . . . Before somebody else does. Tell them about things like Santa Claus and the tooth fairy, but more important, topics such as sex, drugs, abortion, finances, and AIDS. Difficult? Yes, but you will open up the lines of communication and build family-esteem.

My family life is balanced

25. Remember Your Significant Other and Your Parenting Role. When children enter our lives, all too often spouses and significant others receive less and less attention causing disharmony in the family. But a harmonious relationship between the two principal adults in the household is important for a child's self-esteem. Remember to focus your attention on your adult relationships.

If the home environment becomes negative and destructive to all involved, steps for improving this situation are a must.

The negative effects of the divorce process on children have been established. Among these effects are depression, excessive anger and aggression, self-destructive behaviors, decreased academic achievement, juvenile delinquency, thoughts of suicide, and sexual promiscuity. Children of divorce also suffer from low self-esteem because of guilt feelings about being the cause of the divorce, being caught in the middle of conflicts, experiencing dual loyalty, and feeling unloved or abandoned, or both. A disrupted family life can increase negative self-evaluations by fostering feelings of guilt, helplessness, and inadequacy. It can also decrease the child's sense of belonging and cause a loss of security.[10]

If a separation or divorce is unavoidable, make a concentrated effort to leave the children out of the disagreement between partners. Constance R. Ahrons, author of *The Good Divorce* emphasizes this point, "Realize once you have kids, you want to continue parenting even if you divorce."

26. Tell Them What You Do (And Show Them Too.) Let your child know what you do on your job. The League of Women Voters annually promotes a wonderful career awareness day when daughters can go with their mothers to work to see what their mothers do. I believe that all children, boys and girls, should see what their parents do. As your children mature, discuss with them your salary and what "benefits" are.

27. Demonstrate Your Values within Your Family and Community. Demonstrate your values and concern for others on a community level and within your family. Zenger Miller, the national management training company, has five basic principles which I have adapted for family-esteem balance.

1. Focus on the situation, issue, or behavior, not on your child.
2. Maintain the self-confidence and self-esteem of other family members.
3. Maintain constructive relationships with your employees, peers, friends, and relatives.

4   Take initiative to make things better.
5.   Lead by example.

28. Wishin' And Hopin'. Share your hopes and dreams for yourself and family. Let your child know it is okay to dream, that's how miracles begin. I talk to my boys about how some-day I would like to write children's books, and both Ryan and Zachary let me know how great I tell stories. They say, "Come on Dad, you can do it!" I look at them, smile, and say, "Yes, I will, someday."

Once coming back from a walk in the woods, Ryan and Zachary talked about how they wished they had a fort like one we saw in the woods. I said, "Someday we'll build one." They looked at me and smiled, "Yea, someday." Their comments started me thinking hard about the resources of time and ener-gy needed for building a fort. I wanted to help them realize their dreams. We started on the fort the very next weekend. Two weeks later, Ryan and Zachary were in the fort eating pretzels and drinking ice tea. I overheard their conversation:

"This is the best fort in the whole wide world."

"It sure is."

29. Have Your Own Friends. Do things with people you like and have interests in common. In *611 Ways To Boost Your Self-Esteem*, Bryan Robinson and Jamey McCullers suggest you spend time with people who have similar interests and beliefs.

In C. E. Rollins book, *52 Ways To Build Your Self-esteem and Confidence*, Rollins recommends associating with high-esteem people. You'll be inspired, helped, and instructed. "The more you associate with high-esteem people and the more you emu-late their behaviors and mind-set, the more you'll esteem your-self, and the more others will regard you with greater respect."[11]

Not a bad way to build your esteem and set a wonderful example for your child.

30. Get Some QT . . . Quiet Time. Whether it be taking a few quiet moments at home with no one around, reading a book, taking a walk, or going on a weekend retreat, you need that quiet time. If you don't, the pressure and stress will literally kill you. Explain to your child how critical it is for everyone in your family to have quiet time alone. This quiet time or retreat can help develop greater mutual appreciation among family members.

Harry Emerson Fosdick shares this helpful advice:

> "There are two techniques that every man and woman needs to live life. One is the technique of volition, of trying hard, putting your back into it and doing your best. That's output . . . The other is the philosophy of intake, of spiritual hospitality, of the receptivity of the soul to the oversoul, of the open door that lets the highest in. That's intake. One is like the branches of a tree, spreading out. The other is like roots, digging in. Multitudes of people in our modern world are using only the first technique. They are trying hard, and then someday, inevitably, like everybody else, they run into an experience that they can't handle simply by trying hard—a great grief, for example. Try hard? You need intake, too. You need sustenance, you need invigoration from beyond yourself."[12]

There is a tremendous amount of power in a family if the energies are directed in the right manner, that is, as suggested with these 30 activities. Family-esteem is not only developed by parents but also through other family members, through an extended family. Kimberly Bittner describes the strength can come from a family member.

> Lost.
> Lost in a sea of emotions.
> How this came to be cannot exactly be determined—yet it wasn't in an instant.
> It happened over years of shattered hopes, misplaced feelings and altered dreams.
> This came to be through no fault of my own but by a higher and much stronger power.

A power that brought a blessing.

A blessing that would cause empathy, care, resentment, hatred and an overwhelming sense of unconditional love.

This blessing has been a most positive influence on my life. It has veered me toward the right path of life—both personally and professionally.

It has enabled me to see through another's eyes, hear through another's ears, talk through another's mouth, and walk in another's shoes.

This blessing has thrown me into a sea of emotions where I get lost easily—until the blessing itself pulls me onto stable land where I can once again find my path in life.

This blessing is my hero . . .

This blessing is a very "special" person.

This blessing is my sister.[13]

Here is another wonderful example of a balanced self- and family-esteem. It is a story about a courageous boy told through the eyes of his confident, supportive grandmother.

Up to the age of seven Bryan was a normal, athletic little boy. He enjoyed and was very good at all sports, especially soccer and baseball. During the summer of 1990 the doctors at Children's Hospital in Pittsburgh found a tumor growing inside Bryan's spinal column. After an 18 hour operation of opening the spinal column to remove the tumor, Bryan was left paralyzed. Not only is Bryan paralyzed from the rib cage down, he does not have the use of his fingers in his right hand.

The doctors have said that Bryan will never walk again. However, over the past year we have seen some remarkable things happening. There has been some movement in the toes of his left foot and now some movement in his left leg.

Bryan has been mainstreamed into his regular school since the operation and is on the honor roll. He has also been

active in sports again. He has been on a handicapped baseball and volley ball team. He has done horse back riding
and now is currently in a regular karate class. It was recommended that he join this class to help strengthen his
lungs and his upper body.

Bryan is an orange belt with four stripes which means he
will be tested soon for the yellow belt. I am very proud of
the determination Bryan has in this class. He really is a special boy. His attitude through all of this has been wonderful, he has the greatest sense of humor (just like mine I
might add).

I have encouraged Bryan to picture himself being able to
stand and walk with a walker someday. Bryan is a little
ahead of me and said to me, "Grandma, I'm picturing
myself running down a football field with a football."
                        —Darlene Williams
                        Pittsburgh, Pennsylvania

Having high self-esteem means having the power to grow,
to live life more actively, to be more open and responsive to all
that life has to offer, and to be caring of others. As mentioned,
this is important for your child and your family, but as a parent you also need to work on your own self-esteem. Your having a good self-concept is significant in developing your child's
self-esteem. Just as teaching and displaying positive values to
your child involves developing and having your integrity, bet-
tering your child's self-esteem involves building your own
self-esteem.

A mother describes the ill effects when parents don't have
a healthy self-esteem:

I am 37 years old, married, and have two beautiful and
healthy children. I grew up in an alcoholic family. My dad
drank and my mom kept the peace in the family. Needless
to say, I grew up without the hugs and the love that I needed as a child. To get attention, I had to do something bad

in order to get noticed, or some kind of response . . . usually it was a spanking. I in turn married a man who drank and partied. It is said that people often marry just to get away and be loved. Well, I didn't want to have any kids because I was very selfish and I knew that my parents didn't spend much time with me, and I didn't want to treat my kids that way. The bottom line is that we have two children, and I find myself treating them just like my parents treated me . . . like I was in the way.

How you were brought up obviously has a major effect on how you feel about yourself and how you will parent. Here are eight ways to help you with your esteem:

1. Be part of a support group, even if it is an informal group of parents from your school or neighborhood, to share the difficulties of parenting and also the special moments.
2. Forgive your parents and yourself for any shortcomings in your upbringing.
3. Find a mentor or coach, or if need be, therapist.
4. Use the sentence-completion technique as a tool to bring about self-discovery, self-expression and self-healing.
   Complete the following sentences:
   Things I like about myself are. . .
   Things I can do to raise my self-esteem are. . .
   As I learn to simply be myself. . .
5. Do things for yourself.
6. Make a list of your past accomplishments.
7. Share your hopes and dreams with other people.
8. Read more on the subject of self-esteem.

One piece of advice: Be careful not to build your own self-esteem at the expense of your child's. Parents may unintentionally erode a child's self-esteem while improving their own.

One way this happens is when a child has natural talent and the parent tries too hard to cultivate this skill and unfortunately ends up exploiting the child's natural ability and damaging the child's self-concept.

Parents can push their child to the extreme. The parents feel they have a gifted child and push the child to adult and professional levels. The child many times loses out on childhood.

Kathy Horvath tells how she was saddened to hear about her fellow tennis star, Jennifer Capriati, being arrested for drug possession. Horvath said, "She had so much going for her in terms of her talent, but it's unfortunate that she was not a happy person."

For Kathy the story is more positive. Kathy, too, was a tennis champion. I remember seeing Kathy playing tennis in my home town at the age of eight, and at the age of 15, turning professional. She won 10 professional single titles and beat Martina Navratilova in the French Open at the age of 17. She has since left the world of tennis and concentrated on her education with a B.S. in Economics and working towards a MBA. I attribute this difference to the awareness and attention paid by Kathy's parents during Kathy's growing years. They did not sacrifice her esteem for success in the tennis world. They allowed her to grow in all areas and to feel good about it.

There is also another trap some parents fall into—expressing their own desires and aspirations through their child. One place I have seen this is in the pinewood derby races which are a big part of the Scouting program and also the YMCA Parent/Child programs. The youth involved in these programs work on a piece of wood and create a small car to be raced on a track. A wonderful idea, the kids working on a car, feeling proud and excited about their creation! The flaw is that the fathers are often too competitive and they want to win. The fathers work on the cars and do not allow the children to help. The worst case I've seen of this was when a father brought the car in a special holder and when the child wanted to play with this car on the gym floor, the father grabbed the car out of the child's hands and said, "Leave the car alone! Do not touch this car until after the race." In situations like this the values of integrity and good judgment come into play.

When I found myself working with Ryan on his derby car for Cub Scouts, it took great effort to let him sand and paint his own car. I knew most of the other cars would be "father-built," so I explained this to Ryan. I praised him constantly on the work he did on his car. He felt disappointed when he did not win the race, but he feels proud and content about the project he created and completed. Although the car may not be sleek and glossy, he is pleased enough to display his car on his desk in his room. I too am proud of him. He truly was a champion in this event and I let him know it.

In both cases, my son's Cub Scout derby experience and Kathy's early tennis career, the parents and the children were allowed to have dignity. Each person was feeling satisfaction, confidence, and responsibility for behavior. The ultimate goal in this area of esteem-building is to create a synergistic effect for you and your child—both of you building your self-esteem and also the esteem of the family as a supporting unit.

You as a parent must focus on developing wings and roots for your child. Include your extended family in promoting your family esteem. Support and encourage their uniqueness and special interests. Also let your child be a child. The freedom of individuality and the stability of family connectedness means your family members are able to say and believe: "I like myself," "I can do it," "I am responsible for my behavior," "I am loved," "I am an important member (contributor) of this family," "We enjoy being together and growing together as a family unit," "We understand and respect each other," and "I love my family."

If everyone had just one single person in his life to say, "I will love you no matter what. I will love you if you are stupid, if you slip and fall on your face, if you do the wrong thing, if you make mistakes, if you behave like a human being—I will love you no matter," then we'd never end up in mental institutions.
—Leo Buscaglia
American Educator, Author, and
Lecturer on Interpersonal Relationships

4

Talk with Your Child

Children just don't fit into a "to do" list very well. It takes time to be an effective parent when children are small. It takes times to introduce them to good books. It takes time to fly kites and play punch ball and put together jigsaw puzzles. It takes time to listen.
    —*James C. Dobson*
    Founder, Focus on the Family

Communication. Successful relationships depend on open, positive communication. It is essential to communicate information, facts, data, and schedules within the home. Even more important is the practice of family members freely and respectfully expressing their feelings, standards, hopes and dreams, and needs. Communication within a family means adult to adult, adult to child, and child to adult.

Earlier we discussed living our values, which involves respecting others and helping society. We examined esteem, honoring ourselves and our families, and being satisfied. Communication is similar to esteem in that it gives a person dignity, which shows respect for the relationship and builds self-esteem. But communication is different from respect in that it is a skill that shows you care. It is used to express ourselves but, more important, it is a result of loving. Love is not something that comes from communicating, we communicate because we love.

Communicating is the lifeline of a healthy family but it is also one of the most difficult human relations functions. Learning good communication skills is a lifelong process. As a parent, you are your child's initial and major influence and teacher of communication. As the child matures, he or she continues learning in the home environment and also in school. And as your child becomes an adult, communication learning continues from reading books; attending seminars, workshops, retreats, and counseling or therapy sessions; listening to tapes and viewing videos; and life itself, that is, being with people. Some people are naturally excellent communicators but their ability has developed over the years through the help of good parents as heroes and other "teachers." Whatever your level of communication, you can always improve your communications skills. Improving your communication is a voluntary act.

Sue and I felt tense and frustrated due to the stress of dealing with work, raising two children, tending the home, and pursuing personal growth. After 12 years of marriage, we realized we needed assistance in understanding the changes we were both going through. Our own attempts at being open with our thoughts and feelings and empathizing with each other were unsuccessful. We attended marriage-encounter-type retreats and also pursued professional counseling. With time and a counselor's care and concern, we are at a much higher level of understanding. Lew, our counselor, helped us improve our listening skills. He would share his favorite saying which expresses the complexity of good communication:

"I know that you believe you understand what you think I said but I am not sure you realize that what you heard is not what I meant."

Our situation is by no means unique. Communication is probably the number one cause of disharmony in marriages. In a survey of 2,000 women, the two biggest challenges they cited in their marriages were financial difficulties and lack of communication.[1] A New England tombstone humorously illustrates the dire importance of the latter: "I *told* you I was sick Elizabeth."

Communication is also a major factor in raising a connected and bonded family. Dolores Curran, internationally known lecturer, family specialist, and parent, surveyed parents on the most stressful situations in their families. Communicating with children was number five, after lack of shared responsibility in the family, insufficient couple time, children's behavior/discipline/sibling fighting, and economics/finances/budgeting.[2] But more important is that she found that the combination of communicating and listening was chosen as the number one trait found in healthy families. And that's what we really want—to raise a healthy family. Dolores Curran also states that what she found is consistent with the findings of the National Study of Family Strengths and in the work done on the healthy family by Dr. Jerry M. Lewis of the Timberlawn Foundation in Dallas.

Through extensive training, personal life situations, and documented research I have become aware of the great importance of communication and the need for parents to focus on it. The fourth insight I wish to offer you in this book, therefore, is:

Talk with your child and, more important, listen

This fourth insight is a natural addition to the three previous insights I have already discussed. A quick review may be helpful:

1. Understand who your child's #1 hero and role model is—YOU!
2. Know and share your values—demonstrate them to your child.
3. Strengthen your child's self-esteem and family-esteem.

Now, on to communication.

There are four main areas of communication that I call the windows of communicating—talking, listening, non-verbals, and writing. They are windows because it is a two-way process that involves individuals seeing things from different sides or perspectives yet wanting to reach out to another person by speaking, listening, and even touching the other person. To achieve this goal, these windows need to consistently remain open. The first three avenues are necessary when you are with the person. The fourth, writing, is wonderful for those times you are not there with the person or you have difficulty conveying your message orally or you want to give the person something to keep as a memento.

Successful communication is an ongoing, dual-participatory process. A parent must learn the skills of communication—both speaking and listening—and must also be aware of conveying non-verbal messages. Communication involves both conscious and unconscious acts. Positive communication is a conscious seesaw of talking and listening. The unconscious provides the non-verbals which many times display one's real feelings and thoughts.

It is difficult enough to learn and apply these skills for yourself, but again, parents as heroes need to teach their children these same skills. Remember you communicate because you love a person; this needs to be displayed in all four ways.

Before discussing these four windows, the first most essential aspect of developing superior communication, as simple as this concept might seem, is being with the person.

The *New York Times* and CBS News asked more than 1,000 13-to-17-year-olds about their parents, friends, school, and work. Four out of 10 said that their parents often are not available when they need them.[3]

How to be there? Here are my top 10 ways to be with your child, offering opportunities to open the windows for communication.

1. Maximize waiting and driving time by talking and listening to your child.
2. Do chores together such as washing the car, raking leaves, or preparing dinner.
3. Do "nothing" activities together such as taking walks, bike riding, or fishing.
4. Limit TV viewing time for both of you.
5. Use your vacation days as "real" vacation days with your family.
6. Set aside time before bed for talking and reading.
7. Eat at least one meal a day together.
8. Attend as many of your child's school functions as possible.

9. Do things together like visiting museums, horseback riding, and working on puzzles so good times are shared and can be remembered together.

10. Go out for ice cream at least once a week.

After physically being in the presence of your child, developing superior communication involves you and your child talking. Parents as heroes need to focus on these facets of speaking with your child:

- Talk with your child.
- Talk with respect.
- Allow your child to talk.
- Help your child talk by asking questions and open-ended statements.
- Be open to cues from your children if they want to be in special surroundings to talk to you.

Talk with your child

Thomas Gordon, founder of Parent Effectiveness Training, explains that "research has shown that dumb kids come from families in which parents rarely speak to their children unless they're ordering them about. By 'dumb' I don't mean kids who don't do well in school, I mean dumb kids. Studies indicate that the degree to which parents talk to their kids, and the environment they create for them can have a startling impact on the children's IQs—as much as 25 points."[4]

Yes, the everyday opportunities of communicating scheduled activities, homework, and mealtimes are necessary but how a child feels is most important. I learned a great deal in the 50 hours of training I received from the Help Line Telephone Services in New York City. The instructors focus on active listening, a process of reflecting the feelings of the caller. You do not give advice or your personal opinion. Instead, you clarify how the person is feeling about a situation. This is helpful to both you and the other person. The challenge then is to discuss what the person wants to do and what he or she is willing to do for himself or herself.

It is most helpful if you reflect feelings by asking questions such as:

- You appear to be feeling . . .
- It sounds like you are feeling . . .
- I get the impression that you are feeling . . .
- I'm not certain I understand; you're feeling . . .
- As I hear it, you are feeling . . .
- I somehow sense that maybe you feel . . .
- This is what I think I hear you saying you are feeling . . .

These statements show a sensitivity to your child's feelings. If you are correct on the feeling you sense, great! The dialogue continues in a positive fashion. If your feeling word is wrong, don't worry, your child will say "No, I feel . . ." and again, the dialogue continues after this brief clarification by your child.

Below is just a sampling of the many feelings your child (and also you) may experience at various times.

Get in touch with your child's feelings by using the above statements and inserting a word from this list:

afraid, amused, angry, annoyed, anxious, ashamed, bitter, bored, concerned, confused, disappointed, discouraged, embarrassed, excited, frustrated, happy, hostile, hurt, lonely, patient, proud, rejected, relaxed, shocked, tense, trapped, uncertain, unpopular, worthless, zealous.

Of course you want to help your child share his or her experiences and express feelings, but your help sometimes turns to a hindrance or roadblock. Here are 12 of the most frequent roadblocks to communication:

1. Ordering or commanding promotes rebellious behavior.
2. Warning or threatening causes anger.
3. Moralizing or preaching communicates a lack of trust in your child's sense of responsibility.

4. Advising or giving solutions can cause dependency or resistance.

5. Persuading with logic or arguing provokes defensive position.

6. Judging, criticizing or blaming implies incompetency, stupidity, or poor judgment.

7. Praising or agreeing can be patronizing or manipulative.

8. Name-calling or ridiculing causes child to feel unworthy or unloved.

9. Analyzing or diagnosing stops child from communicating for fear of distortion or exposure.

10. Reassuring or sympathizing causes child to feel misunderstood.

11. Probing and questioning results in children replying with non-answers, avoidance, half-truths, or lies.

12. Diverting, sarcasm or withdrawal stops openness from child when he or she is experiencing a difficulty.[5]

Remember, talk with your child and be aware of the times where you should just reflect feelings and not "parent." Initiate conversation and be in tune with how your child is feeling.

Talk with respect

At a parenting seminar, I made the suggestion to parents to carry a small cassette player on themselves to record conversations with their children. A few of the parents in the audience gasped. These parents thought about what they say to their children during a typical day:

Your child's morning may start with a comment from you like this, "Come on, get up. Don't be so lazy."

Your child gets dressed and your response is, "You're wearing that!" While your child is changing clothes you give your child a warning, "You just took that shirt out of your closet, don't you dare put it in the laundry."

Your child makes an attempt to eat breakfast and share a few words with the family when suddenly you blurt out,

"Don't talk with your mouth full." This is quickly followed by "Don't be a pig—use a napkin. And make sure you put the milk away."

You peer in the bathroom and yell out, "How many times have I told you to clean the toothpaste out of the sink?"

You look at the clock and scream out, "Come on slow poke, get up to the bus stop and pick up your feet when you walk."

Before you know it, your child is coming home and is greeted with your afternoon request "Get your muddy shoes out of the kitchen." The verbal lampooning continues while your child does his or her homework, "How can you mess up on these easy math problems?" Your child shows signs of anxiety but you don't see this and you continue with your demands "Stop chewing gum like that." After finishing the work, your child goes outside for a breath of fresh air and hears your voice again, "Close the door when you go out—we do not live in a barn."

It is dinner time and you offer some helpful instructions, "Go wash your hands again and do it right." At the dinner table, your nagging persists, "Use your silverware, we are not animals, and sit up straight."

The evening concludes with final orders, "Get off the phone now—my call is more important." Your child retreats into the bathroom and hears your voice following closely behind, "Brush your teeth right, not like a two year old, and put the towel back where it belongs."

Humorous? Definitely. True? Quite possibly.

The question is "Do you talk to your friends, neighbors, and relatives like that?" I doubt it.

Talking with respect means a minimum of basic courtesy and politeness. Remember you communicate in a respectful manner because you love your child. You are building your child's self-esteem and setting the parent-as-hero example for respect.

Just think if instead of comments such as those mentioned above, you said something like this to your teenager, "Thank you very much for coming to dinner—it is a pleasure to have you here this evening."

After the initial shock wears off you will be pleasantly surprised at your child's future responses.

In regards to talking with your teenager here are offerings from 13- to 18-year-olds on the 10 statements parents should never say to their kids, which may prove helpful in composing a more positive and decent conversation with your child. Remember these are statements you can do without.

Because I said so—that's why!
What's the matter with you?
Shut up!
You're older—you should know better!
How many times have I told you . . . ?
No ifs, ands, or buts about it.
Now what?
When I was your age. . .
Now you listen to me!
I don't want to hear anymore about it![6]

Allow your child to talk

"My father and I had words this morning," said a small child, "but I didn't get to use mine."

James D. White, author of *Talking with a Child*, says that many children have little chance for actual conversation with adults. People talk to them, not with them.

Allow your child to talk. There are three ways to help your child express himself or herself. The first is to assist your child in acquiring good language skills. This includes detecting and correcting any speech or hearing impediments, assisting with proper grammar usage, and editing your child's language relating to slang words and derogatory or racist remarks.

The second way to help your child talk is to encourage your child to ask questions. The most efficient way for your child to gain information and to improve academic performance is by asking questions to get answers he or she needs. The way to encourage your child to ask questions is, first, to make it a pleasurable and helpful experience when he or she does ask a question. This will give your child confidence to ask a question the next time. The second way is for you to ask questions. Again it is you being the example that your child will follow.

The third way to help your child express himself or herself is asking your child's opinion. A big part of a child's self-esteem is rooted in the feeling that his or her ideas are valuable and meaningful to a parent.

Students at a Madison, Wisconsin, high school suggested that parents, "Give us a chance to disagree with you without telling us that we're 'talking back.' Never stop talking to us. You're the only ones we can count on for reassurance and love."[7]

Help your child talk by asking questions and open-ended statements

Communicating with your child means initiating conversations even if your child appears to be non-talkative. Sometimes it means stepping out of your comfort zone to start a conversation. It is a risk but remember heroes are risk-takers.

Looking back, one young adult says she would have talked to her mother about a problem with sex, "if only there had been a word, a 'lead' on my mother's part . . . the floodgates of sharing a painful problem would have been released."[8]

As every parent quickly learns, it is difficult to start a conversation with your child when they come home from school if you just ask "How was school?" A curt "Fine" or "Okay" usually is the reply.

Ask how school was today but follow up with additional questions such as "What is new in history class?" or "How is the school football team doing?" Be persistent but not overwhelming with your questions. And most of all be sincere.

Another way to start your child talking is asking about his or her favorite: animal, book, candy, cartoon, color, dessert, food, friend or classmate, hero (celebrity, sports star, or teacher), McDonald's food, memory, movie, music group, physical activity, quiet activity, school subject or class, song, sports team, television show, video or computer game, or wish list item. Showing interest in what a child likes is a sign of caring.

Also discuss everyday experiences with your children and their interpretation of the news, life, school. Ask them "What do you think about . . . ?"And a more in-depth session might include a "What would you do?" exercise discussing potential situations in which your child needs to think about the different options of how he or she might act. Participating in this practice type of role-playing is helpful in dealing with precarious situations outside the home.

The need for special surroundings

While raking the fallen leaves and pine needles, Ryan and Zachary asked me to join them in their fort. Very astutely, I stopped to think before I answered (I'm learning too). My first response was leading towards a "no." Then I realized this was a special invitation—they were inviting me to come into their special place. I said, "Sure, let's go." Well, the next twenty minutes was a wonderful time of hearing about what goes in and around the fort, some interesting tidbits about their friends, and even information on traits and actions of their teachers. It was a floodgate of conversation opened up mainly because my sons felt comfortable in their territory, a place where I was the outsider. I was not only treated kindly in their abode but was informed of many happenings in their lives that I might not have had the opportunity to hear otherwise. As your child grows older, this comfort zone of a special place might be the mall, a ball field, even a car as Marion Bond West shares in this story about her older son.

My husband Gene and I and my twenty-four-year-old son Jeremy were having lunch at a popular restaurant when, suddenly, without warning, the conversation between Jeremy and me took a sharp, unexpected, angry turn. I hate to admit it, but I've often lost my temper with this one of mine and this time I did it again. I snapped back at him loudly. People stared. Our friendly waitress's smile froze. My husband glanced down beneath our table as though he might crawl under it. Jeremy looked at me in disbelief. Soon I was dissolved into tears. "Why can't we get along, Jeremy? Do you know how much I love you?" I asked, a familiar helplessness overtaking me. Finally, we left the restaurant.

Outside, we stood awkwardly, silently. Suddenly, Jeremy broke the silence. "Hey, Mom, you want to ride in my new corvette?" He said, smiling openly, confidently, waiting for my answer.

Still blowing my nose, I answered curtly, "No. No, thank you." Jeremy jumped into his car and roared off.

As Gene and I drove home, he said, "Marion, Jeremy can't express love the same way you do. He was telling you that he loved you when he asked you to ride in his new car. It was his way of reaching out."[9]

All of us need someone to reach out to and this is especially true for youth. Remember if you are not there, or if you are unwilling to start conversations and join your child in their world, they will look elsewhere for suitable or unsuitable company.

And the greatest of compliments coming from an open relationship is that your child (or in this case, grandchild) may ask you, the hero, for advice.

At a local high school graduation, Frank Maendel, valedictorian of the Webutuck High School offers this insight.

A while back I asked my 89-year-old grandmother what advice she would have for a graduate of the '90s, and what she said was very interesting.

Make sure, she said, that you take enough risks. She said

whatever you do, do it 200 percent. She said to enjoy the good times to the max and smell the roses along the way. Finally, she said, find a purpose for your life bigger than yourself and fill it with meaning. I thought about all that and I realized something. After four years of high school we've spent more than 5,000 hours in the classroom. And yet, just as important as the academic lessons learned are those which life has taught us. About taking risks.

The fear of failure keeps many from taking risks and trying the seemingly impossible. But if you never take a chance you'll never know whether you would have succeeded or not, and sometimes that's harder to live with than failure. Risk is the spice that makes life taste interesting and fuels the desire for future endeavors. As you leave for the years ahead, don't forget to take a chance.[10]

A true compliment to the grandmother for the open lines of communication she has with her grandson. Also her reply offers good advice for life and advice for parents as heroes in the area of communication. Take a risk. Take a risk by talking to your child more than you might feel is necessary and allow your child's opinion to be voiced.

Listening

When giving my seminar on "100 Ways To Build Your Child's Self-esteem," numbers 76 through 89 are the same: listen, listen, listen, listen, listen, listen, listen, listen, listen, listen, listen, listen, listen, and listen. A bit extreme? Not when I share the story about the adolescent who attempted to commit suicide because nobody listened.

It was shocking news. Ann, who was only 11 years old, made an attempt to commit suicide. I was aware of the rising statistics. Suicide is currently the ninth leading cause of death in the United States overall, and the third leading cause of death among adolescents, resulting in 30,000 total fatalities each year. Of these cases, more than 5,000 involve children. In addition, about 500,000 people attempt to kill themselves each year (12% children). One researcher asserts that children try to kill themselves at a rate of one every 90 seconds. While these statistics are significant, some clinicians believe suicides are underreported by as much as 10%, and the number of adolescents who kill themselves may be two or three times higher than reported.[11] Fortunately this 11-year-old who came from what seemed like a good family did not succeed in her attempt.

But the more I thought about it, the more I realized that there was were some problems within this family. The parents were separated, in the process of divorce. In addition, her mother was working full time and was out during the evenings attending social events. The mother was also in the process of developing a new romantic relationship. Throughout that time period, the child must have felt abandoned. This child who had in the past been paid a considerable amount of attention and who was now faced with these dramatic family changes taking place, needed someone. She needed someone to listen to, not only for the everyday happenings and circumstances in her life, but more important for her feelings relating to the major changes that were taking place.

The attempted suicide seemed a drastic act but the child must have felt that the other signals of "distress" she displayed to her parent went unnoticed and that this hopefully would do the trick. It did! The parent and child began to communicate again. The parent realized she had to pay more attention to the child's needs, by trying to listen and to understand her concerns and desires in this period of her child's growth. Unfortunately, it took such a drastic measure by the child for the parent to realize that there was a problem. This dreadful occurrence could have been avoided with better communication between them expressing feelings, concerns, disappointments, and, of course, expectations. But communication also involves more than just talking, it includes listening.

Listening is important to learn. It helps you understand where your child's thoughts and ideas come from—their perception of the situation.

". . . Listening is an art not easily come by, but in it there is beauty and great understanding. We listen with the various depths of our being, but our listening is also with a pre-conception or from a particular point of view. We do not listen simply; there is always the intervening screen of our own thoughts, conclusions and prejudices. We listen with pleasure or resistance, with grasping or rejection, but there is no listening. To listen there must be an inward quietness, a freedom from the strain of acquiring, a relaxed attention. This alert yet passive state is able to hear what is beyond the verbal conclusion. Words confuse, they are only the outward means of communication; but to commune beyond the noise of words, there must be in listening an alert passivity. Those who love may listen, but it is extremely rare to find a listener. Most of us are after results, achieving goals, we are forever overcoming and conquering, and so there is no listening. It is only in listening that one hears the song of words."[12]

Listening goes beyond hearing what we want to hear, and keeping an ear out for what might help us. Debra Lane recounts a lesson she learned about teenagers and listening.

I was the new junior varsity coach for the girl's field hockey team. As my first week of practice neared, I became tense. I questioned whether I could do this. My biggest concern was: Could I relate to these teenagers, remain in control, and also produce a winning season?

I found the first three weeks to be a period of adjustment and testing. I became aware that not only toddlers, such as my son, will try to see how far an adult will be pushed; so will 13- and 14-year-olds. I was being tested constantly. There was Cortney, who didn't want to practice, yet expected to be put in the games because of her superior athletic skills. And Jennifer, who often became ill, coincidentally during the more difficult practice drills. Although they were not my children, I would demonstrate one of the rules for parenting—firmly showing kindness. I believed it was important to show them respect, even if people commented that "they're only teenagers."

Working with thirteen teenage girls was quite the task. But an even more difficult dilemma was reprioritizing my initial goal of having a winning season. That goal became secondary. I was being given the opportunity to do more than be just another coach for this team. These girls, as difficult as they were to deal with, were reaching out to me. I quickly became aware of the stresses these girls were facing—ongoing peer pressure, questions on dating, challenging school work, and unfortunately for some, a difficult home life.

At the beginning of the fourth week, I made the decision to give my all in teaching the necessary skills and strategies for playing field hockey to the team members, being firm but fair when situations warranted it. I also knew that I needed to respond to these high school girls with open ears and an open heart. I began to develop a rapport with the girls that was positive, close, and pleasurable. I realized that besides being the trainer for these girls, I was someone that could be "there" for them. I could take the time to listen, to listen to what each of them had to say, not only to her ideas and concerns as a hockey player, but also to her concerns as a teenager going through one of life's difficult growing periods. This was a time in the lives of these girls when everyday happenings could be confusing or stressful. I would take the small risk of allowing myself to be the someone they might need to talk to. The season ended with a mediocre record including a win over our arch rival, but more important was knowing I was there for these youth. I knew I had fulfilled a significant role for them when one of the players asked if I would be back next year. I told her I was not sure. She replied, "I hope so. You're a good listener."

When asked about their problems with parents, teenagers most often cite "not being listened to." Really listening is not always easy. The National Institute of Mental Health offers advice on how parents can help keep communications open. Some of the following suggestions may help you:

- Give your undivided attention when your teenager wants to talk to you.

- Try to listen calmly, even though there may be a difference of opinion.
- Develop a courteous tone of voice in communication.
- Avoid making judgments.
- Keep the door open on any subject.
- Permit expression of ideas and feelings.
- Encourage positive self-worth.
- Be aware of how you treat other children in the family.
- Make an effort to say nice things.
- Hold family conferences.

It is not realistic to expect complete harmony between the generations. Nor is it pleasant to live through a period of bickering and strain, no matter how temporary.[13]

There is power in listening, the power of building a strong, lasting bond and also strengthening a person's self-esteem and worth. Parents as heroes have access to this power whenever they are willing to put their energies into it.

When someone deeply listens to you it is like holding out a dented cup you've had since childhood and watching it fill up with cold, fresh water.

When it balances on top of the brim, you are understood. When it overflows and touches your skin, you are loved.

When someone deeply listens to you, the room where you stay starts a new life and the place where you wrote your first poem begins to glow in your mind's eye. It is as if gold has been discovered.

When someone deeply listens to you, your bare feet are on the earth and a beloved land that seemed distant is now at home within you.[14]

In a values guide I've created, I dedicate an entire section to *Be Listening*. Here are some of my recommendations:

- Be listening to family, friends and children, this alone will lift them to greater heights.
- Be listening to the birds' songs echoing in each new day along with the opportunities that await for being there for your child.
- Be listening when your child shares their feelings, whether it be feelings of loneliness, despair, or happiness.
- Be listening to world and regional news, but more important to your child's call for help.

It is also necessary and important to practice listening for your own self-growth and understanding, just as it is important to build your self-esteem. Here are my suggestions:

- Be listening to a preacher, teacher, or counselor, and evaluate their wisdom and how it relates to you and the action you can take in your role of parent.
- Be listening when other responsibilities—job, family, finances or health—are calling.
- Be listening when others—teachers, parents, co-workers, supervisors and children—want to teach you something.
- Be listening to the Higher Power that speaks within you for strength, patience, and love.

And number 90 at my seminar is "And listen some more."

Non-verbals

I was only four years old, but I remember Mr. Fredericks. He was a friend of the family and would visit the laundromat where my mother worked. Mr. Fredericks was a big man with gray hair, but what stood out the most was his smile. Whenever I saw him, he smiled and said, "How's my Sunshine doing today?" It was pleasurable seeing an adult smile at me. It felt reassuring and positive. I remember this man for his kind and sincere smile. How wonderful it is for a facial expression to convey a feeling of love.

Dale Carnegie shares a one word principle in his book, *How To Win Friends and Influence People*. It is "Smile." Carnegie, known for his world-wide courses including "Effective Speaking and Human Relations," believes smiling is essential in all human relationships. He describes the importance of a smile in this wonderful poem.

The value of a smile at Christmas

It costs nothing, but creates much.

It enriches those who receive, without impoverishing those who give.

It happens in a flash and the memory of it sometimes lasts forever.

None are so rich they can get along without it, and none so poor but are richer for its benefits.

It creates happiness in the home, fosters good will in a business, and is the countersign of friends.

It is rest to the weary, daylight to the disadvantaged, sunshine to the sad, and Nature's best antidote for trouble.

Yet it cannot be bought, begged, borrowed, or stolen, for it is something that is no earthly good to anybody till it is given away.

And if in the last-minute rush of Christmas buying some of our salespeople should be too tired to give you a smile, may we ask you to leave one of yours?

For nobody needs a smile so much as those who have none left to give![15]

A smile is so helpful, yet it is under-utilized by most parents. Are you smiling much at your child? How about your teenager? Remember to smile at your child at all ages.

Smiling is just one of the non-verbals we project to our child. Pats on the head or back, hugs, and hand gestures such as a thumbs up sign are wonderful ways to communicate love and caring to your child.

Non-verbals can also convey anger, sometimes in harsh

ways. Physical violence is an example of a destructive non-verbal. Hitting a child says to the child that you do not respect him or her and also that you approve of violence as an option. Find alternatives and other outlets for yourself if you find yourself feeling pushed to the limit.

Be aware of what feelings you send to your child via non-verbals. Also look to your child for how he or she is expressing himself or herself to you. Gary Smalley is one of America's best-selling authors. He has written seven national best sellers on relationships and is a popular speaker on personal and family relationships. During his seminars, he focuses on something he calls "closing the spirit." He says, "A person is made up of three ingredients—spirit, mind, and body. The spirit of a person is your innermost being; it's who we are, as a person. The mind is our mind, will, and emotions; it's where we feel, where we talk with someone or give in or resist in our will. The body is all of our physical make-up, hormones, and skin."

Gary says you "can wound someone's spirit and they start closing on you. When you close the spirit of your children they close you out. They deny your values. They want to put distance between you."[16]

Closing your child's spirit (or your own) can mean closing mind and body also. It may produce anger, resentment, frustration, and confusion, in essence, leading you (or your child) to become critical and hostile to others, particularly loved ones. It greatly hinders the development of successful relationships and a healthy family.

I can recall a time that I closed my son's spirit and closed it tightly in a matter of minutes. Ryan and I were out working in the yard on a warm spring afternoon. We were cleaning up the remaining leaves from the fall. We were using rakes and a wheelbarrow to transport the leaves from our yard into the wooded area behind our home. I decided to make a little game of this chore by giving Ryan a ride in the wheelbarrow full of leaves. We both enjoyed this little game for quite a while. Then he began to "tease me" by taking the wheelbarrow into the woods trying to hide it from me. This was fun for a while then I repeatedly asked him to bring the wheelbarrow back. He refused, thinking we were still playing a game. I clearly and firmly requested him to retrieve the wheelbarrow. He ran to where it was and attempted to push it even further into the bushes. I became angry and pulled the wheelbarrow out of the shrubs "accidentally on-purpose" braising Ryan as I pulled it out. He was not physically hurt but his spirit was. He became angry. No, it was more like FURIOUS! I was astounded how infuriated we had become with each other within a few minutes. I quickly realized that what I had done was wrong and I needed to rectify this dilemma. But my first attempts at discussing what had taken place and why were futile—his emotions had taken over any "rational" thinking. I continued pursuing forgiveness and warmth until he reluctantly gave me a hug, which was a sign that our dispute was nearly over. My sincere and persistent intentions and communication aided in restoring my son's trust and affection for me. What was needed was genuine consideration and regard for Ryan, treating him with respect. Gary Smalley describes this genuine love and respect as "The Five Keys That Open a Closed Spirit." They are:

1. Becoming gentle, demonstrating tenderheartedness.
2. Understanding what the other person has gone through, listening carefully not only to what is said but how it is said. Honestly looking at what has caused their anger.
3. Acknowledging that the person is hurting and admitting when you have been offensive.
4. Touching the other person gently.
5. Asking for forgiveness.[17]

With this seemingly minor incident, I was made aware that each and every one of us has this "spirit," and how we act and react towards each other can either facilitate the opening of one's spirit or compel the person's spirit to close.

Although my wife and I have had our share of our sons' crying, whining, and uncontrollable fidgeting in church, attending church has become special in a new way. We come to church with a new outlook. We expect the time in church to be one of reflection and love, and our sons have realized our intentions. During the service, both Ryan and Zachary will look at us and give us a big smile. We return this gesture with an even bigger, warmer smile. They will also move close to us and give us hugs. We again return the hugs. We feel the family spirit and delight in it.

Writing

Two parents who are out of town on business more than 100 nights a year explained to me how they use phones and faxes to communicate with their children. Once their 13-year-old daughter was faxed permission to cut her hair—a bit extreme and quite impersonal, but it is one of today's alternatives of communicating orally. Besides the normal writing of letters and cards, faxes, E-mail, and on-line computer services are becoming everyday occurrences, but this example is the exception rather than the rule. The writing I am discussing is that of letters.

Writing is a form of communication that reaches out with a variety of emotions. Sometimes it is desperation, sadness, appreciation, or love. If used constructively, writing can be powerful and therapeutic.

Children write notes to parents, and parents write letters to their children. But sometimes children are reaching out to others in letters. Many letters sent to helping agencies or written in diaries depict desperation. Younger children express it briefly and to the point. Older children share more details and write personal feelings.

"Please pray that my daddy comes back to my mommy and me."
             —John, California

"The divorce I'm going through is really tough for me. I'm hoping you can help me age 8 and my sister age 5!"
             —Katie and my sister Erin, Alabama

"I'm fifteen years old and I need a lot of help. I was sexually abused by a friend of the family a year ago. I'm having
a hard time dealing with that. I'm also having nightmares
of my past that I don't remember much of. I just wake up
in the middle of the night crying. A couple of weeks ago I
tried to kill myself by cutting my wrist. This is twice I've
attempted suicide in four months."

—Karen, Oklahoma

Sadness is often expressed through diaries or written stories. This is a story written by a senior from Maria Regina High
School for a Youth Writing Contest. She begins by describing
how her 11-year-old brother was hit by a car and placed in an
Intensive Care Unit.

Well, Ace, you made it through one more night. When we
got to the hospital early Monday morning, you were having a CAT scan done. We were told we could see you after-
ward. You came back in cardiac arrest, with the doctors
giving one last scramble for your life.

My mind was frantic. You cannot die now, Mike! You have
too much to live for! What about the guitar lessons you
were going to take—the band you were going to start with
Matt and Vinny? What about the basketball team—you're
the starting center. Wait, Mike, don't go. I love you too
much to lose you. Keep fighting, please!

Well, Ace, I know you did what you could. You could only
fight so long with so much against you. It was the worst
moment in my life when I heard "He's gone."The room
spun. I felt detached from my body, as if the pain of this
startling reality was too much to bear. I wanted to die too,
to be with you, to make sure you were okay.
After they took out all the tubes and monitors, the doctors
let me in to see you once more. I felt that your soul was
close. I wanted to shake your shoulders and have you open

your eyes. Instead, I gave you a kiss and rested my face against yours, willing to do anything to bring you back. The only thing I could do was let you go.

Mike, I know you're still with me. I know you're helping me get on with my life. I learned much from you. You taught me to live one day at a time, to appreciate everything that comes along, to laugh and have fun, to be honest, to accept people for what they are. And while 11 years is a short time, we filled them with so much happiness that can never be lost, even now.

I really miss you, Ace, but I know that you are still with me, and I know we will see each other again.

I love you, Jenn[18]

Parents also use this medium to express their feelings. Our family is a "writing" family, particularly my mother. She is appreciative of special events, trips, and gifts, and she sends heartfelt letters and cards thanking us for our caring. Mom wrote touching letters when I graduated from high school, when I went to Florida State University (FSU), when I married, and when our two sons were born. I cherish each and every one of these cards.

Over the years I have kept many of the special letters and cards from friends and family. When I began to write this section of the book, I pulled out the cardboard box of memorabilia including these letters. I was surprised to find that during my college days at FSU, I wrote to my father numerous times. I found the first letter I got back from dad.

Dear Steffen,
What a surprise!
First I was scared to open your letter because you never write to me and I thought maybe something happened and you didn't want to tell your mother first.

After sharing some things about his health, my younger brother, and asking about my grades, he closed with this:

> It is very nice that you already have a gift for my upcoming birthday, but no money can beat this "emotional happiness" gift of your letter.
> Thanks a million.
> Love,
> Dad

I had forgotten about these letters and reading them now impacted me greatly. It helped me remember my father's sense of humor and his love for me. I was glad I kept the letter from my father because it helps me remember him in a positive light. It adds much to my image of him as a hero.

Carol Kuykendall, mother of three teenagers, describes a similar story, but from the parent's viewpoint.

> The moment I'd dreaded was finally here. It was time to say good-bye to Derek, our oldest, in a college dormitory fifteen hundred miles from home. For months I had anticipated this scene, wondering what I could say that would appropriately leave him with a feeling of confidence and support. As it turned out, I barely muttered more than a quick "good-bye."

> "It's two o'clock ," Derek exclaimed as we finished unpacking his belongings in that tiny dorm room. "I'm supposed to be at a meeting right now!" With a quick circle-of-family hug, he was out the door. From his window, I watched him walk away and felt a stabbing sense of separation . . . and frustration. I hadn't said anything.

> With tears in my eyes, I pulled a sheet of paper from his desk and jotted down three family messages we'd tried to pass on to our children as they grew up: "Remember, Derek: 1) There is no problem so big you can't solve it; 2) We always love you; and 3) You are never alone. Love, Mom." I tucked the note under his pillow.

A few days later, Derek phoned. "Thanks for your note, Mom. I put it on my wall so I can remember what you said when I'm feeling low."

Carol points out that sometimes a written message—short and sweet—is more appropriate than a spoken word (lecture) because it gives a person something to hold on to.[19]

Within a family, love means communication. It helps instill values. It promotes self- and family-esteem. Communication is a demonstration of love. Parents as heroes love their family. M. Scott Peck in *The Road Less Traveled* describes love as "a form of work or a form of courage. The primary form of work that love takes is the giving of attention. The primary way we give our attention is through listening."

Listening—such an essential aspect of successful relationships! Good listening makes use of ears, eyes, and emotions. It takes energy and time. Lou Holtz, winning coach in the 1988 NCAA National Championship, once said, "Success comes from listening. I've never learned anything by talking." How true of the many happenings in life, particularly in parenting.

Be there for your child and keep the lines of communication open. Don't stop communicating with your child, however difficult it may be. If you do, you are abandoning him or her, which can lead to the death of your relationship with your child. Parents as heroes reach out time and time again. If you don't, this is when your child searches for a new "hero," positive or negative. Again we communicate because we love.

Mother Teresa of Calcutta is a wonderful example of a hero of love. We will never be as giving on a scale as large as she has reached, but Mother Teresa gives us hope. Many people hearing Mother Teresa speak ask her "What can I do?"She tells these individuals, "Go home and love your family."

Love your family by communicating in an open and positive manner. Kenneth Baldwin, psychotherapist, counselor, and author tells parents about the "Seven L's." There are three harmful "L's" and four helpful "L's." The three harmful ones are lectures, labels (insults), and lickings (corporal punishment).

The four helpful "L's" are listening, loving, limits, and letting go. He says, "Paying attention to what your child is saying is one of the best forms of caring you can give. Listening demonstrates respect and enhances the child's inner security."

The second is loving, that is, caring plus appropriate touching. The third is setting limits. And the fourth is letting go. He states, "If we have built healthy relationships with our children, we can feel relatively secure about our ability to influence their behavior when they are away."[20]

Open the windows of communication and keep them open. Be there, make yourself available. Give your child your attention. Talk to your child. Ask sincere questions relating to how your child feels. Encourage your child to ask questions. Let your child talk. Allow your child to give his or her opinions. And perform the most heroic act of all . . . listen. Listen with your ears, eyes, and heart.

Remember that listening heals. When someone you love has difficulties, listen. When you feel terrible that you can't cure them, listen. When you don't know what to offer the people you care about, listen, listen, listen.
         —Dr. Bernie Siegel
         Author, How To Live between Office Visits

5
Examine Your Child's Environment

It takes a whole village to raise a child.
—African Proverb

Environment. Your child's environment is the things and people that surround him or her throughout the day. It consists of your child's physical surroundings at home, the neighborhood, school bus, school, malls, friends' homes, house of worship, ball fields, studios, and so on. It also includes your child's peers, other adults, television, books—essentially whatever your child hears, sees, tastes, touches, and smells. This environment affects your child in positive, negative, or sometimes even in neutral ways.

Today's national discussion on setting up orphanages for homeless, poor, or abused youth demonstrates a renewed awareness of the importance of a good environment and upbringing. It focuses on the poor parenting environment these children are being raised in. The two opposing solutions, putting these children in orphanages or keeping the children in detrimental homes, do not acknowledge the fundamental problem. A major focus needs to be placed on raising families appropriately and responsibly. Parents of troubled youths are not being taught this major responsibility of caring for their child nor the skills to do this.

I don't propose to solve the dilemma of orphanages versus the welfare system in this book. But I do want to help you

113

become aware of those environmental factors affecting your child's growth and to suggest what you can do as parent as hero. First, it is necessary to acknowledge the basic notion that your child's environment significantly influences what your child learns and how your child acts. Even if you try to do everything right, many other outside factors will leave impressions on your child. Ann Beattie shares this thought:

> Do everything right, all the time, and the child will prosper. It's as simple as that, except for fate, luck, heredity, chance, the astrological sign under which the child was born, his order of birth, his first encounter with evil, the girl who jilts him in spite of his excellent qualities, the war that is being fought when he is a young man, the drugs he may try once or too many times, the friends he makes, how he scores on tests, how well he endures kidding about his shortcomings, how ambitious he becomes, how far he falls behind, circumstantial evidence, ironic perspective, danger when it is least expected, difficulty in triumphing over circumstance, people with hidden agendas, and animals with rabies.[1]

As outlandish as some of these might be, there is some truth to these influences. One tragic example is the case of Elizabeth Glaser, who was infected with the AIDS-causing virus in 1981 when she received blood transfusions during the birth of her daughter Ariel. Ariel died in 1988 because of this. Another example of uncontrollable events in our lives is what happened to Reverend Scott Willis and his family.

The car just ahead of Reverend Willis swerved around a steel bracket that had rattled loose from a semitrailer on I-94. Willis wasn't so lucky. The bracket punctured his mini-van's gas tank, engulfing it in acrid smoke and fire. Willis and his wife, Janet, survived. Their six youngest children did not.

Some circumstances we cannot control, but there are some we can. There is much you can do in the capacity of parent as hero when it comes to monitoring your child's environment.

This brings us to the fifth insight I want to share with you. But before I reveal it, let's review the other four:

1. Understand who your child's #1 hero and role model is—YOU!
2. Know and share your values—demonstrate them to your child.
3. Strengthen your child's self-esteem and family-esteem.
4. Talk with your child, and, more important, listen.

As in all of the other areas of values, esteem, and communication, you have to take an active role in the area of your child's environment. The fifth insight therefore is:

5. Examine your child's environment, determine what you can do to enhance it or, if necessary, change it, and teach your child about choices and consequences that relate to your child's well-being.

Everyone seems to be worried about our youth. Whether we look at violence, alcohol or drug use, sexual activity, sexually transmitted diseases, or school failure, youth face many pressures and choices that deeply disturb us.

In the face of these problems, we often spend time and energy trying to figure out who's to blame or how to "fix" the problems. Yet the problems only seem to get worse, or they are replaced with new ones. We reach the point where we begin to wonder whether anything will work.

Using a study of 50,000 youth in grades six through 12 from 111 communities in 25 states, Search Institute has identified 30 "developmental assets" that young people need to grow up healthy. Young people who have many of these assets in their lives are much more likely to make positive choices—and much less likely to make negative ones.[2]

As a parent, we should obviously strive for developing characteristics and behavior that are positive in our children. Our goal would be for what Search Institute calls "positive youth development" to be achieved. But what does this behavior look like? Search Institute has described "the well-being of our youth" as encompassing four criteria:

1. Having 20 or more of 30 assets. These assets consist of 16 external assets—things that surround youth with support, boundaries, and constructive activities and 14 internal assets—commitments, values, and skills that guide youth in their choices.
2. Having two or less of 10 deficits, factors inhibiting teenage development.
3. Being involved in prosocial behavior at least one hour per week, that is the desire or intent to promote the welfare of others.
4. Having two or less of 20 at-risk indicators.[3]

It is worth looking closely at the full listing of assets, deficits, prosocial behavior, and at-risk indicators and analyzing how these relate to your child's environment and to your role in dealing with that environment.

Parents as heroes have a tremendous effect. You might think that you have little control over your child's various environments, but in reality you as a parent are the most influential environment. Your role relates to values and role modeling, self- and family-esteem, and communication. The 20 criteria for the parent as hero discussed in Chapter 1 are particularly important here when you look at the assets, deficits, at-risk indicators, and prosocial behavior. Before examining these Search Institute characteristics in detail, let's take another look at the 20 criteria for your role as hero.

1. You accept a responsibility.
2. You take care of your children.
3. You provide the moral example.
4. You set basic values.
5. You model positive behavior when dealing with difficulties.
6. You show your child is important.
7. You meet the challenge.
8. You are the right kind of hero.
9. You admit your imperfection.

10. You treat your child with respect.
11. You will be imitated by your child in all you do.
12. You change your behavior as needed.
13. You are self-disciplined.
14. You have a significant role.
15. You are a role model.
16. You have the most lasting effect.
17. You build your child's self-esteem and your family connectedness.
18. You form the world.
19. You shape the future.
20. You love your child.

Too many times parents say that controlling their child's environment is out of their hands. This is untrue—you are still the major influence. As we discuss different environmental aspects outlined by the Search Institute, for example, I would like you to stop and focus on how you can enhance the environment or, if necessary, change it, but this is secondary. As you read through this chapter, I invite you to primarily focus on your role as hero using the 20 principles or criteria I have suggested. To help you with this task I have listed the appropriate principle or criteria of hero following the various topics covered in the chapter. Let's look carefully at the significant role you play in developing the well-being of your child.

Now lets examine the four positive characteristics described by the Search Institute one by one and see how some of my 20 principles apply to supporting those characteristics. We will begin by looking at the 30 assets—first the external assets, then the internal ones.

1(a). Having 20 or more of the following 30 assets. These assets consist of 16 external assets—things that surround youth with support, boundaries, and constructive activities. . . . These are:

1. family support
2. parent(s) as social resources

3. parent communication
4. other adult resources
5. other adult communication
6. parent involvement in schooling
7. positive school climate
8. parental standards
9. parental discipline
10. parental monitoring
11. time at home
12. positive peer influence
13. involved in music
14. involved in school extracurricular activities
15. involved in community organizations or activities
16. involved in church or synagogue[4]

Looking at the list you will see that many pertain to you the parent—you being a major environment in your child's life. Of the 16 assets above, at least eight relate directly to what you do as a parent; numbers 4 and 5 relate to other adults; and the remaining six deal with school. As you consider the importance of building these assets in your role of parent as hero, be mindful of Hero Principle #14: **You have a significant role.**

1(b) Having 14 internal assets—commitments, values, and skills that guide youth in their choices. These are:

1. achievement motivation
2. educational aspiration
3. school performance
4. homework
5. values helping people
6. is concerned about world hunger
7. cares about people's feelings
8. values sexual restraint
9. assertiveness skills
10. decision-making skills
11. friendship-making skills
12. planning skills

13. self-esteem
14. positive view of personal future[5]

These 14 internal assets are direct results of the establishment of values and the building of your child's self-esteem. Again you have the opportunity to play a major role in establishing these internal assets.

This is reflected in Hero Principle #6: You show your child is important.

2. Having two or less of these 10 deficits, factors inhibiting teenage development, which are:

1. alone at home—being at home two hours or more per day without an adult
2. hedonistic values—placing high importance on self-serving values
3. TV overexposure—watching television three hours or more per day
4. drinking parties—frequently attending parties where peers drink
5. stress—feeling stress or pressure "most" or "all of the time"
6. physical abuse—report of at least of one incident of physical abuse by an adult
7. sexual abuse—report of at least one incident of sexual abuse
8. parental addiction—report that a parent "has a serious problem with alcohol or drugs"
9. social isolation—feels a consistent lack of care, support, and understanding
10. negative peer pressure—having most close friends involved in chemical use and/or are in frequent trouble at school[6]

This category of deficits includes influences or environments that you cannot completely control such as television and parties. But still, your example and your behavior, especially as they relate to physical or sexual conduct, have a tremendous impact on your child's well-being. And overseeing your child's other activities and experiences is needed to avoid deficits such as stress and television overexposure. During your child's teenage years, you will need to find a balance between enforcing certain rules and being flexible in others. The parent as hero focuses on these two criteria—Hero Principle #13: You are self-disciplined and #12: You change your behavior as needed.

3.   Being involved in prosocial behavior at least one hour per week, that is the desire or intent to promote the welfare of others.[7]

Your efforts to help your child become active in some volunteer work or community service will yield positive behavior, including the development of the internal assets previously mentioned. And one of the best ways to spark an interest in your child to volunteer is for you to set the example, remember Hero Principle #11: You will be imitated by your child in all you do.

4.   Having 2 or less of the 20 at-risk indicators. The 20 at-risk indicators are:

1.   frequent alcohol use
2.   binge drinking
3.   daily cigarette use
4.   frequent chewing tobacco use
5.   frequent use of illicit drugs
6.   sexually active
7.   non-use of contraceptives
8.   depression
9.   attempted suicide
10. vandalism
11. group fighting
12. police trouble
13. theft

14. weapon use
15. school absenteeism
16. desire to drop out
17. driving and drinking
18. riding and drinking
19. seat belt non-use
20. bulimia[8]

These at-risk factors play a substantial role in the well-being of your child. Obviously these are times when you may not be present to oversee your child's environment. During these times, critical judgments and their consequences are in your child's realm and require astute decision-making skills. Although numerous hero criteria apply, focus your energies on Hero Principle #4: You set basic values.

To many, these criteria may seem strict or even "old-fashioned" (or some people may say not strict enough), but they represent a good set of guidelines to aid in creating positive youth development.

Only 10 percent of students met what the Search Institute study identified as minimal standards for overall well-being. How do you get your child into this 10 percent? The main action is being the parent as hero.

What you do and what you say are relevant in how your child acts while at home and also in surroundings where you are not present.

Let's take a look at some specific areas of your child's environment where you may not always be present.

- School
- Television, movies, and music
- Malls

School

Children are facing more severe problems in school today than students did in the past. According to the California Department of Education, the top seven discipline problems in 1940 were:

1. talking
2. chewing gum
3. making noise
4. running in halls
5. getting out of turn
6. wearing improper clothing
7. not putting paper in the trash can

The agency reported the top present problems as:

1. drug abuse
2. alcohol
3. teen pregnancy
4. suicide
5. rape
6. robbery
7. assault

In a recent survey of 65,193 sixth through twelfth graders, 37% of the students said they don't feel safe in schools; 26% of the girls and 49% of the boys said they were hit during the previous year at school; and 55% of the students in grades 10-12 said they know weapons are regularly in school.[9]

In another questionnaire of 93,455 youth ages 12 to 18, 74% said drinking is as big a problem as, or bigger than, sex and drug use in the school.[10]

A third survey of 12,272 high school students in 50 states and the District of Columbia found that 27% of them had thought of suicide, 42% had been in a fight during the year preceding the survey, and 26% carried a weapon.[11]

In working with a national children's magazine, I see many letters from youth ages 8 to 14. I'm shocked when I read the letters of extreme depression and threats of suicide expressed from 11-year-olds. For me, it makes these statistics come alive.

What can a parent do to make your child's learning environment most productive and safe? It is a three-step process.

1. Examine your child's school environment and become involved in school functions and your child's learning process.
2. Take the initiative in selecting your child's learning environments.
3. Teach your child about choices and consequences.

In addition to my work with teachers and students, I talk with teacher aids at various elementary schools. In their role, they quickly learn the "inside story" regarding what happens in a typical suburban school. They know the problem children, the "better" teachers, and the uncaring parents. They are aware of the importance of a child's home life and also of the link between parents and teachers in providing the best coordinated effort for a child's learning.

From these experiences and from what learning experts say, becoming involved may be one of the most important things parents can do to ensure the quality of their children's education. Whether it's volunteering for school projects or helping with homework, the more parents get involved, the more they learn about the schools and about their kids' academic progress, says Kathryn Whitfill, president of the National PTA.[12]

It is not only vital to be involved in the early years but also throughout the teen years. Remember Hero Principle #1: You accept the responsibility.

A report by Child Trends says parental involvement in schools drops off sharply after students enter high school. The percent of students whose parents were moderately or actively involved in school declines from 73 percent for ages 8-11, to 67 percent for age 12, 57 percent of age 13, and 50 percent for ages 16 and above.

The report stated that students whose parents have little school involvement were twice as likely to repeat a grade and three times as likely to have been suspended or expelled.[13]

Caring and becoming involved are essential keys to your child extracting the most from school time. Know what's going on with teachers, school work, and peers. Parents and teachers working together is vital. Here is a poem that expresses this concept.

Unity

I dreamt I stood in a studio
And watched two sculptors there.
The clay they used was a young child's mind
And they fashioned it with care.
One was a teacher—the tools he used
Were books, music, and art.
The other, a parent, worked with a guiding hand
And a gentle loving heart.
Day after day, the teacher toiled
With thought that was deft and sure
While the parent labored by his side
And polished and smoothed it over
And when at last, their task was done
They were proud of what they had wrought:
For the things they had molded into the child
could neither be sold not bought.
And each agreed they would have failed
If each had worked alone.
For behind the teacher stood the school
And behind the parent, the home.

—Author Unknown

To take this concept one step further, as the opening quote of this chapter states, "It takes a whole village to raise a child." What you, your school, community, and congregation do are all relevant. Search Institute provides a poster which describes "240 Ideas for Building Assets in Youth." They offer suggestions for parents, community organizations, schools and congregations.

For the external asset of parent involvement in school, Search Institute offers eight ideas.

For parents/families:

- Make it a point to talk with all of your child's teachers during the school year.
- Regularly ask your teens what they are learning in school. Offer to help with homework in appropriate ways.

For community organizations:

- Coordinate activities with the school so parents don't have to choose between school events and community events.
- Provide activities for children to free parents to participate in parent meetings.

For schools:

- Have teachers personally contact each family at least once during the school year.
- Form a parent advisory committee to give input into school policy decisions.

For congregations:

- Don't schedule congregational activities that conflict with important school activities for parents.
- Encourage parents to take any concerns they have to the school.[14]

If you discover your school system is a negative learning atmosphere or harmful to your child's well-being, request changes. Communicate your thoughts and feelings to other parents, teachers and principals, the school board, even local police and political leaders. If your efforts do not get the action you want, focus on Hero Principle #2: You take care of your children. And then think about changing schools or even home schooling.

After only three months in school, Thomas Edison returned home one day in tears because his teacher had called him stupid and put him in the back of the class. When Edison's mother learned what had happened, she confronted the teacher. Then she withdrew her son from school and taught him at home where she was able to foster his natural curiosity.

Many years later, Edison said of his mother, "Her encouragement helped me to believe in myself and develop my creative potential."[15]

Besides school, look for positive experiences in camps and other extracurricular programs. I will mention a few of the innovative programs around the country. Check around your area for other peripheral camps and learning environments.

Children of the Earth in Winnipeg is one among eight native "survival schools" that have sprung up across Canada in response to the failure of traditional education to stem high dropout rates for Indian students.

Junior Entrepreneurs Initiative at Babson College in Wellesly, Massachusetts, is a summer camp for inner-city teens working to translate street smarts into business know-how.

Builders Club, a five-year-old service organization in Greenville, Alabama, is funded by the state and actively supported by the local Kiwanis Club. Builder's Club is open to all middle school students willing to work on service projects during breaks and at lunch, as well as after school.

You as a parent have a voice in your child's education and learning atmosphere. Be assertive in this area. Positive youth development involves locating a good learning atmosphere for your child, but it also means teaching your child responsibility for his or her behavior. It means teaching your child about choosing. It is important for your child to know that the choices your child makes determines the direction and quality of his or her life experience. Your goal of parent as hero is assisting your child in focusing on a positive transformation from childhood to young adulthood, not allowing any type of deterioration. Your children need to discover their power to determine what they think and feel, and how they respond. How do you do this? One way is to take another look at the list of criteria for parent as hero particularly focusing on Hero Principle #3: You provide the moral example.

There is an article by the actor Iron Eyes Cody about an Indian youth which vividly points out the power of choice, particularly in the area of youth and drugs. I recommend you write for this article and ask for it to be sent to your child— your child may be more likely to read it if it comes in the mail. Write to Guideposts Ministries, 39 Seminary Hill Road, Carmel, New York, 10512 and request a copy of the article, "Words To Grow On" by Iron Eyes Cody.

Teens are faced with choices as they mature. As depicted in the story above, there are consequences when a wrong choice is made. I remember a children's game (and also a game show) called Truth or Consequences. It gives the choice of telling the truth or paying the consequences. This is an important principle to teach your child.

We've already stressed the importance of honesty as a value, but Josh McDowell and Bob Hostetler show how truth relates directly to our concerns of cheating, stress, and drugs.

Josh McDowell and Bob Hostetler surveyed 3,795 youths ages 11–18 and asked them 193 questions. Here are a few of their findings:

- 66 percent said they had lied to their parents or another adult in the last three months. Almost that many (59 percent) had lied to their peers.
- 45 percent watched MTV at least once a week.
- 55 percent said they are confused.
- 50 percent said they are stressed out.
- 46 percent said they are always tired.

McDowell's and Hostetler's stress that it is vital for our children to understand truth. Their study indicates that when our children do not accept an objective standard of truth, they become:

- 48 percent more likely to cheat on an exam
- two times more likely to watch a pornographic film

- three times more likely to use illegal drugs
- six times more likely to be angry with life
- two times more likely to be lacking purpose
- two times more likely to be resentful

It is important to teach our children that being honest protects from guilt and provides a clear conscience; protects from shame and provides a sense of accomplishment; protects from the cycle of deceit and builds a reputation of integrity and a "good name"; and protects from ruined relationships and provides for trusting relationships.[16]

Honesty, a value we already discussed, is taught by you, parent as hero, by setting basic values (Hero Principle #4) and being a role model. Remember Hero Principle #15: You are a role model.

School is a major component of your child's environment and development. Make sure you have a say in what this surrounding looks like. Obviously you cannot control all elements of this environment but you, parent as hero, have a tremendous effect on your child's values and esteem, both of which are essential to offset any negative aspects of your child's environment. And if your child's environment is intolerable or does not meet your standards, change it. This recommendation relates not only to schools but to the next subject, television programming.

Television, Movies, and Music

By the time a youngster is 12 or 13, he or she will witness approximately 8,000 murders and more than 22,000 assorted acts of violence.

By the time kids turn 18, they will spend 17,000 hours watching television, 11,000 hours of school, and 1,160 hours at the movies.

The three most heavily advertised cigarette brands—depicted by Joe Camel, the Marlboro Man, and the fun couples of Newport—have captured 86 percent of the teen-age market.

Does the world of television affect a child's behavior and upbringing? Absolutely!

A number of studies have shown that violent television shows and movies have a negative effect on viewers. There are no studies indicating today's violent movies somehow contribute to well-being.

Bo Pittman, one of the MTV's creators and a former chairman, has long understood the power of this medium. "The strongest appeal you can make . . . is emotionally. If you can get their emotions going, (make them) forget their logic, you've got 'em. At MTV, we don't shoot for the 14-year-olds, we own them."[17]

You do not have to look only at such national news programming about O. J. Simpson or Tonya Harding to see the major influence of violence today on television. Violence is in every community. In Saugerties, New York, a 13-year-old girl and her 15-year-old boyfriend are accused of brutally strangling the girl's grandmother. The youth are only 13 and 15! Police say the teens put the grandmother's body in the trunk of her car and carried on normally. They bought pizza and went to the mall.

As a parent you should voice your discontent to executives of major television networks and film makers about harmful programming. But the best way to control what your child is subjected to is controlling what is being watched and listened to in your home. Be assertive in controlling what is being viewed in your home and also offer positive alternatives.

Along with television, video games are part of most teen's environment. And as with television, there is a considerable amount of violence in video games. Because it is likely that there is some similarity in the effect on an individual's aggressive behavior from viewing violent television programs and playing violent video games, those concerned with the effects of video games on children should take note of television research. The consensus among researchers on television violence is that there is a measurable increase of from 3% to 15% in aggressive behavior after watching violent television. A recent report of the American Psychological Association claimed that research has demonstrated a correlation between viewing and aggressive behavior (Clark, 1993).[18]

Concern over violence is a national concern, an educational topic, and a parenting matter.

What Can Be Done about This Violence?

With the obvious violence in schools and society as a whole, a major focus by school officials and public TV is on violence. PBS has coordinated the development of a four-part series "What Can We Do About Violence?" with Bill Moyers and Peggy Noonan. The series is part of public TV's two-year anti-violence campaign and focuses on solutions to crime.

One of the objectives of Healthy People 2000 is to reduce fighting among teenagers by 20% by the year 2000.

Schools teach conflict resolution as a way to deal with violence. William Kreidler, former classroom teacher and leading expert in conflict-resolution education, offers these recommendations for the classroom, but they can be adapted for home.

1. Recognize that conflict is a normal and natural part of life and can be positive.
2. Create a "peaceable" classroom community.
3. Lay your groundwork.
4. Set up how-to steps for handling conflicts.
5. Clarify consequences of physical fights.
6. Focus on the positive.
7. Plan a varied and active conflict resolution program.
8. Set a good example.
9. Be patient.
10. Have fun.[19]

It is necessary for you to teach coping skills to your child. Focus on Hero Principle #5: You model positive behavior when dealing with difficulties, and also Hero Principle #9: You admit your imperfection.

Coping skills such as walking away, using humor, being patient, teaching about people's differences, staying cheerful, being kind, and continuing to do his or her best will help in dealing with violence and conflict. There are also numerous comprehensive conflict-resolution programs. Here is a listing of six organizations offering curriculas.

1. Children's Creative Response to Conflict (CCRC) (914) 353-1796
2. Community Board Program, Inc. (415) 552-1250
3. Consortium on Peace Research Education and Development (COPRED) (703) 273-4485
4. Educators for Social Responsibility (ESR) (617) 492-1764
5. National Association for Mediation in Education (NAME) (413) 545-2462
6. Peace Education Foundation (800) 749-8838

Malls, Family Events, and Community Programs

Malls are the social gathering places for today's teens. They have become the teen centers for this generation. And that's not all bad. It's a safe environment, for the most part, if your child is with responsible friends.

Make sure you know who your child is associating with, especially if you are concerned about drug use. *How To Help Your Children Avoid Drugs* by Little League Baseball of Williamsport, Pennsylvania, offers many helpful hints for preventing drug abuse. Two of them are:

*   Monitor and guide their friendships. Pay close attention to friends; talk to them and get to know them. Make sure other parents supervise when they are in someone else's home.
*   Create a home environment that helps children resist drugs. Home should be a haven for children, a place where they can feel safe and happy—not a place from which to escape. Lack of communication at home drives children to look for it elsewhere, and children who spend little time at home are more likely to use drugs on a daily basis.[20]

Concentrate on providing a positive home environment

including respect for your child. Focus on Hero Principle #10: You treat your child with respect.

Parents can affect a child's environment. Create an age-appropriate environment at home. As your children become adolescents, they want a place to hang out. They may choose the mall, a street corner, or a playground . . . or, if it is inviting enough, they might choose home.

One of the most memorable times, or as I call them "unforgettables," of my childhood was the summer time. It was special because of a decision my parents made—one that I did not realize was a major sacrifice until I was out of high school. My parents chose to purchase a pool—an above-the-ground circular pool with a deck encompassing it. Looking back, my parents' incomes did not exactly permit such a purchase, but they managed a payment plan that made the purchase of this pool possible. My brothers and sister and I almost literally lived in the pool. It was our summer vacation—we did not take any major trips, as our friends and neighbors did. We enjoyed the time in the pool immensely. It was pure and simple fun. We enjoyed a safe and pleasurable atmosphere because of a deliberate effort on my parents' part to manage our environment.

As I entered high school, there were two places I usually could be found—at a friend's house where we "hung out" and played pool for hours on end or else I was at the basketball court near my house. Day or night, my friends and I would "shoot hoop."

What are your child's interests? Is there a positive environment which might be available to him or her? How about creating one?

A mother who understood her 15-year-old's need for a place to have friends over got creative. She transformed a section of her basement, which was used for storage, into a lounge type room with sofa and ping pong table. It became her son's own space where his friends could gather.

Begin to think about a setting your child may be interested in—maybe it's another parent's home, a YMCA, a health club, the library, a music store, a school, a park, or nature center.

Help your child find a place that promotes and nourishes your child's personality and interests.

In these settings, mentors and other adult role models come into the picture. When I was at the basketball court with friends, there was a police officer named Terri. Terri would stop and talk with us. After about six months, Terri asked if we would be interested in playing basketball in a gym. Terri had taken the initiative to reserve a school gym so we could play indoors in the winter. Mentors and teachers will be discussed more in chapter 9, but know that the settings your child is in may offer opportunities to know other adults and see positive role models.

Besides creating an environment and monitoring where your child is (and with whom), a third option is enjoying family time together, whether it be at home or within a structured program.

A recent Time/CNN poll of adults showed that 69% of the people surveyed said they would like to "slow down and live a more relaxed life."Great! What a terrific way to begin finding enjoyment, pleasure, and contentment. Bring out the cards, Monopoly game, and chess board—take a walk, make popcorn, go camping—have fun, become satisfied, and find joy in things you like to do, but make sure you share them with your child. I'm sure the delight you show will filter down and stimulate your child to find like activities for himself or herself. Your efforts in creating enjoyable experiences at home offers fun times as well as opportunities to build your child's esteem, both self and family. Remember Hero Principle #17: You build your child's self-esteem.

Besides activities at home, your family can have wonderful experiences participating in organized programs in the community.

One of my most fulfilling experiences while working at the YMCA was with the parent/child programs—Indian Guides and Indian Princesses. I've always enjoyed working with children and this program offered a great opportunity for experiencing "families in action."

Indian Guides and Indian Princesses are two national programs that many parents (especially fathers) may not be familiar with. They are YMCA-sponsored programs for fathers with children ages five to eight. These programs assist in developing a close bond between father and child, within each family, and as a group within the whole program. The program allows the parent and child to build trust and respect, opens lines of communication, offers many activities to participate in together, and fosters an atmosphere of unconditional love. In my experiences working with a group of over 600 fathers and their children, I noticed a real connection, warmth, and vibrancy developing between the parent and child. One special event that contributed to this spiritual connection was the "Induction Ceremony," where new participants were inducted into the program and "old" members renewed their "pledge" to each other. It was touching and sincere—it made this special bond real and significant.

Dr. Michael H. Popkin, founder and director of the national program Active Parenting, confirmed this attachment in an editorial he wrote in his newsletter. Dr. Popkin shared a poem he wrote for his father for his 70th birthday. The poem referred back to when Harry G. Popkin (the father) participated in the Indian Guides program with Michael.

Do you remember the Indian Guides?
I was just seven, and you signed us up
for that father-son club. And we beat the tom tom
That called those meetings together
every month for seven years.
And we each had our Indian name.
You were Big Red Fox.
I was Little Red Fox.
And we'd end each meeting with a solemn vow:
"Pals forever, son" you'd say
And I'd answer, "Pals forever, Dad."[21]

Looking back 33 years, Dr. Popkin recalls those times together as special. A warm connection was formed during those events and activities, and over the years it was nurtured and sustained for a lifetime.

The experiences you have with your child are meaningful during the activity and also valuable in establishing a long-lasting relationship. Remember Hero Principle #16: You have the most lasting effect.

A Loving Environment

It is vital to provide an environment of love: love that disciplines and also understands. According to authors Gary Smalley and John Trent, love has two sides.

It's essential that we learn to balance love's hard and soft sides every day if we want to communicate to others the deepest, most meaningful kind of love.

Hardside love is doing what's best for another person regardless of the cost. Held in balance, it's the ability to be consistent, to discipline, to protect, to challenge and to correct.

Softside love is a tenderness that grows to be the same color as unconditional love. When held in balance, it manifests characteristics like compassion, sensitivity, patience, and understanding."[22]

Focus daily on Hero Principle #20: You love your child.

There was a movie back in 1980 called *The Earthling* starring William Holden as Patrick Foley and Ricky Schroder as 10-year-old Shawn Daley. In the story, Patrick is dying and is heading out to land that his now deceased parents owned and grew up on, land that is "hidden" in a far-away valley in Australia. Shawn is traveling with his parents in a recreational vehicle. As they stop for lunch near a cliff, Shawn's parents are hurled with the vehicle over the edge, as he watches. Patrick witnesses this tragedy and realizes he needs to help Shawn get back to civilization, but he does it in a "tough love" manner. He is hard on the boy, all the while trying to teach him how to survive and have confidence in himself.

It was a tough love. Patrick was teaching Shawn to think

and act. Underlying this hard teaching we discover his love for the boy. After Patrick and Shawn make it to their destination, Patrick is sitting by a fire when Shawn shouts to him, "I hate you. I really hate you."

Patrick replies, "I know. I know you do."

Patrick puts out his hand, realizing the boy is reaching out and needs affection. Shawn takes his hand. Patrick tells him about the death of his own parents. He gives Shawn a hug. Shawn says, "I love you. I love you."

Patrick says, "I never told my father that. I couldn't touch him. Don't ever be ashamed of love. Show it. Always show it."[23]

Patrick dies the next day.

There's a Latin proverb that relates to parenting. It says, "It is the part of a good shepherd to shear his flock, not to skin it." Parent as hero needs to know how much of the hard love and how much of the soft love to give, to find that important balance. Almost every day you face trials in parenting so keep in mind Hero Principle #7: You meet the challenge.

The challenges you will face include the negative behavior and crisis situations created by your child's environment. These crises, however, can also be seen as opportunities. Two Chinese symbols combine to form the word for crisis. One of the symbols is for danger and the other is for opportunity.

A crisis can be an opportunity to teach your child about the world—different religions, cultures, habits, even the negative aspects of society—crime, abuse, and suffering. No one can run away from differences and problems. Now is the time to assist your child in seeing where he or she may fit in—what part does he or she want to play. Help your child see this as a time for transformation—a part of growing up. Your job of parent as hero is to help make this amazing transformation positive and to convey that this is not a time for deterioration.

When your child's environment becomes a negative agent, focus on internal growth, motivation, and contentment. It is important to point out that if you focus on instilling values, building your child's self- and family-esteem and keep communication lines open, the effects of a negative environment are greatly reduced. Again, it is your job to offer your child the best environment but also, knowing detrimental situations will arise, to give your child the tools to deal with them. The instruments are strong values, high self-esteem, good communication skills, and decision-making confidence.

Remember you are helping to develop a unique individual but also a contributing member of society. A parent as hero makes a major contribution by realizing Hero Principle #18: You form the world.

Being parent as hero, you protect, but also inspire, enable, teach, and empower your child. Another one of Search Institute's 240 Ideas For Building Assets In Our Youth is to instill hope. Hope is described as youth having a positive view of their personal future.

For parents:
- Inspire hope by being hopeful.
- Don't dismiss teens' dreams as naive.

For community organizations:
- Encourage youth to name fears of the future so they can be addressed.
- Help youth set personal goals that inspire hope.

For schools:
- Encourage and support students in pursuing their own dreams.
- Expose students to positive role models with similar backgrounds.

For congregations:
- Learn to identify signs of depression and offer professional counseling.
- Pass on to young people the hope that is integral to your faith tradition.[24]

Hero Principle #19: You shape the future.
And you are doing this by employing the five insights:

1. Understand who your child's #1 hero and role model is—YOU!
2. Know and share your values—demonstrate them to your child.
3. Strengthen your child's self-esteem and family-esteem.
4. Talk with your child and more important, listen.
5. Examine your child's environment, determine what you can do to enhance or, if necessary, change it, and teach your child about choices and consequences that relate to your child's well-being.

You have to be protective but not overbearing. And you need to teach the powerful act of choosing and explore with your child how consequences come into the picture. The environment influences your child greatly. You control only so much of your child's environment, but if you are following Insights 1, 2, 3, and 4, you have less to worry about here.

I was reminded of the enormous number of environmental elements bombarding my children every day when we went to New York City on a bus trip to attend a show at Radio City Music Hall. As we walked in Times Square, our two boys were presented with sirens, police, large television screen, signs for "girlie shows," corner vendors, a band set up on a street corner, hurried people, and traffic. Our children saw these things and we talked about them and some of their negative connotations, but our ultimate goal for bringing our sons to New York City was the show which demonstrated positive aspects. At the show we were greeted with artists, a spirited show, and a holiday message. The day presented a barrage of environmental aspects, both negative and positive.

You as a hero have the honor and the challenge of protecting your young child, setting a positive example as they grow, organizing learning experiences both formal and informal, explaining the negative aspects of life during adolescence, and loving your child throughout life. You set the stage for an atmosphere of learning, growing, understanding, and decision-making.

Remember Hero Principle #8: You are the right kind of hero. What you say and what you do are the cornerstones of your child's personality, esteem, and value system and they equip your child to handle challenging environmental forces with confidence, courage, and know-how.

*Perhaps the greatest social service that can be rendered by anybody to the country and to [hu]mankind is to bring up a family.**
—*George Bernard Shaw*
British Dramatist, Critic

* (and to bring up one's family in a loving and truthful environment!)

SECTION 2
Parents, You Are the Light— A Mirror

Heroes: Celebrities, Famous Individuals and Characters, Altruistic People, and Humanitarians

After reading through the first five chapters, you know by now you are your child's number one hero and role model. This is a very prestigious position and also a demanding one, one that we, parents as heroes, can find overwhelming. There are two important points to remember.

First, you cannot and will not be perfect. Artist Georgia O'Keeffe offers this advice, "High standards are realistic goals; perfectionism is self-abuse." Do the very best you can and continue to learn and grow in this position of parent.

The second point is a corollary of the first. There will be traits, characteristics, and values that your child will copy from you which are not as positive as you would like. Jan Blaustone in her book *The Joy of Parenthood* acknowledges this difficulty: "It is as rewarding to watch your child imitate your best traits as it is painful to watch her or him imitate your worst."

Be your best in the position of parent as hero, but realize your child also has other role models and heroes including

141

celebrities, famous individuals and characters, altruistic people, and humanitarians.

Let's examine each of these categories of individuals and see how they measure up to the definition in chapter 1: "A hero performs a deed that provides a meaningful, positive change in someone." More important, let's discuss why some of these characters are seen as heroes and how we can help our children select and use positive role models in promoting their own self-worth and individuality.

6

Heroes or Idols?

Hollywood Celebrities and Sports Stars

Fame is the thirst of youth.
—George Byron (1788-1824)
English Poet

Dressed in dark clothes, he sneaks around the randomly stacked barrels of toxic chemicals at the Axton-Cross storage compound. He carefully ventures to the back of the old, brick factory, climbing a loading ramp and onto the rooftop of an adjoining building, always being alert for the police—and also the "enemy." As he peers into the open window, he sees rows of sophisticated machinery. Voices from the floor below make him hesitate to go in. Instead he decides to head back to base camp with the information he's discovered. He scampers across the roof, jumping onto the 18-wheeler truck. Jumping off the truck he runs along the river hoping the search boat does not see him. Fleeing through the woods, he continually looks back, checking to see if anyone is tracking him. He runs swiftly to his home, out of breath, pleased that he was not captured. Plopping down in his living room with a drink, he turns on the television and waits for his favorite program to come on.

A scene from *Rambo*, James Bond, "Cops"? No, this scene is a memory from my past. I was about 12 years old playing at the factories near my house. My favorite television series was the detective show "Man from U.N.C.L.E." and my hero was David McCullum. I idolized and imitated him by venturing down to these old factories with my brother and prowling around pretending to reenact scenes from the show. All we did was climb around these buildings; we never damaged or took anything.

That was over 25 years ago. Does television have an impact on youth? It did back then, and it does even more so today. The actors, actresses, rock stars, and professional athletes seen on television and other forms of media are considered by some to be heroes. If we refer back to my definition of hero, which is "a hero performs a deed that provides a meaningful, positive change in someone," then these personalities are not heroes. I think a better description for them is idols or the new term, icons, but changing their title by no means diminishes their influence on youth. Are they affecting your child in a negative manner? Only if their actions glorify destructive behavior such as violence, substance abuse, or crime.

Let's take a look at these popular present-day idols realizing that new icons are rising to the surface every day. Although the individuals may differ from generation to generation, the answers to the following three important questions about celebrities and athletes are the same for 20 years ago, today, and five years from now:

Who are these heroes? Why are they idolized? What can our youth learn about or from them?

Television and celebrity status

It was probably in the 1950's when actors and actresses starting gaining an elitist status as movie stars and celebrities. People began idolizing them. Jayne Mansfield, Marilyn Monroe, Elvis Presley, James Dean, and others began to make their debut as Hollywood stars. Television became the catalyst for raising performers to almost a level of gods and goddesses, inspiring the public's worship.

Richard Schickel, writer and film critic, answered the question, "What do you think is the most important, or interesting, or overlooked way in which America has changed since 1954, and why?" His reply was, "Television, which in 1954 was a black-and-white and sometime thing, quickly revealed the private lives of famous people. In the wink of history's eye it granted us instant access to, instant intimacy with these strangers. The rest of the media had no choice but to follow if they were to remain competitive."[1]

Television. How important is it in our lives? There are over 93,100,000 households with TVs; in other words, 98% of U.S. households own at least one TV set! Television is becoming so influential that a recent editorial cartoon showed a small child, with her mother, looking at the TV and saying "Daddy."

Not only has television become a babysitter or a type of parent, but children use television to search for heroes. Dr. Slaby, a developmental psychologist at the Education Development Center in Newton, Massachusetts, who studies the effects of television on children states, "From as early as you see young children being able to control the television dial, we see boys and girls selecting different programming." He adds that boys generally choose programs with strong male characters and girls choose programs with strong female characters.

Television is a major part of our lives and will continue to be extremely influential as technology progresses to the point where the television will become the main source for information and entertainment in your home.

What types of shows are popular on television? The answer to this is obviously changing daily. Even the network executives spend a great deal of time and money researching what our youth and adults may be interested in. Here is a partial list of All-Time Top Television Programs:

"MASH" (last episode) viewed by 50,150,000 households on 2/28/83; XVII Winter Olympics (second Wednesday) viewed by 45,690,000 on 2/23/94; "Super Bowl XXVIII" viewed by 42,860,000 on 1/29/94; "Cheers" (last episode) viewed by 42,360,000 households on 5/20/93; "Super Bowl XXVII" viewed by 41,990,000 households on 1/31/93; "Super Bowl XX" viewed by 41,490,000 households on 1/26/86; and "Dallas" (Who shot J.R.?) viewed by 41,470,000 households on 11/21/80.[2]

It is evident that shows that allow viewers to get to know the actors, actresses, and sports stars intrigue people. What these characters and athletes do on television sets an example for the viewers to imitate. Many times you may find your child imitating a television character's behavior and mannerisms. Sports stars in particular are very popular with our youth. In fact, in one survey athletes rank very high as heroes of teens. Here are the results of this survey of 7,500 teens in the seventh through twelfth grades. The survey asked the question, "Who are your heroes?"

Athletes/sports stars	31.1%
Friends	14.9%
Parents	11.7% *
Dad	11.3% *
Siblings	11.0%
Actors/actresses	10.2%
Mom	10.1% *
God	8.5%
Musicians	7.8%
Michael Jordan	6.8%
Cartoon Characters	6.3%[3]

* Note: These three represent parents and total 33.1%, the highest category, as previously described in chapter 1.

Let's take a look at some specific people youth are idolizing. *The World Almanac and Book of Facts* was annually surveying youth about the Heroes of Young America up until 1991. Here are the results of their 15th Annual Poll:

The top hero was General H. Norman Schwarzkopf, commander of Operation Desert Storm. The second place finisher and "Top Heroine" was actress Julia Roberts, star of *Pretty Woman*. Third through tenth places were these people, in order: George Bush, Michael Jordan, Barbara Bush, Mariah Carey, Kevin Costner, Oprah Winfrey, Madonna, and, tied for tenth, Paula Abdul and Supreme Court Justice Sandra Day O'Connor.

Heroes of past years were Paula Abdul (1990), Michael Jordan (1989), Eddie Murphy (1988), Tom Cruise (1987), Bill Cosby (1986), Eddie Murphy (1985), Michael Jackson (1984), Sylvester Stallone (1983), Alan Alda (1982), and Burt Reynolds (1981 and 1980).[4]

A summary of the people making news is completed by *People Weekly* in the beginning of each year. The magazine picked the 25 most intriguing people of 1994. They were: 1) Bill Clinton; 2) Tim Allen; 3) O. J. Simpson; 4) The Pope; 5) Princess Diana; 6) Gerry Adams; 7) Shannon Faulkner; 8) Michael Fay; 9) Whitney Houston; 10) Ricki Lake; 11) Vinton Cerf; 12) Michael Jordan; 13) Heather Locklear; 14) Jim Carrey; 15) Tonya Harding; 16) Jeffrey Katzenberg; 17) Nadja Auermann; 18) Aldrich Ames; 19) Christine Todd Whitman; 20) James Redfield; 21) Andre Agassi; 22) Liz Phair; 23) Power Rangers; 24) John Travolta; and 25) Newt Gingrich.[5]

People Weekly also does a Best and Worst Dressed listing of celebrities. A recent issue selected these people:

10 Best Dressed: Sarah Jessica Parker, Barbara Walters, Boyz II Men, Barbra Streisand, Tom Hanks, Heather Locklear, Daisy Fuentes, Lloyd Bentsen, Tracey Ullman, and Hugh Grant.

10 Worst Dressed: Hillary Rodham Clinton, Ethan Hawke, Christina Applegate, Susan Lucci, Howard Stern, Brett Butler, unpronounceable singer formerly known as Prince, Fergie, Kim Fields, and the Arquette Family[6]

There are many other surveys and lists of stars including *Good Housekeeping's* Twenty-Sixth Annual Most Admired Women Poll, and Fourteenth Annual Most Admired Men Poll. The results are:

1. Barbara Bush
2. Mother Teresa (18 years in the top 10; she was #1 last year)
3. Hillary Clinton
4. Oprah Winfrey
5. Marilyn Quayle
6. Margaret Thatcher

7. Rosalynn Carter
8. Erma Bombeck
9. Diana, Princess of Wales
10. Katherine Hepburn

1. Billy Graham (#1 for three years in a row; his 14th time in top 10)
2. George Bush
3. Jimmy Carter
4. Bill Clinton
5. Pope John Paul II (14th year in top 10)
6. Dan Quayle
7. Norman Schwarzkopf
8. Colin Powell
9. Ronald Reagan
10. Bob Hope[7]

A recent poll by Louis Harris and Associates for America's favorite film stars has Clint Eastwood topping the list, followed by the late John Wayne, Mel Gibson is third, Harrison Ford is fourth, and Tom Hanks is number five. The top female star is Whoopi Goldberg at number nineteen.[8]

For *Sports Illustrated's* 40th anniversary in 1994, the September 19 anniversary issue featured and ranked 40 individuals who have most dramatically elevated and altered the games we play and watch. Here is the list, selected by the magazine's editors and writers:

1) Muhammad Ali, 2) Michael Jordan, 3) Roone Arledge, 4) Jim Brown, 5) Billie Jean King, 6) Pete Rose, 7) Marvin Miller, 8) Larry Bird and Magic Johnson, 9) Arnold Palmer, 10) Mark McCormack, 11) Carl Lewis, 12) Wayne Gretzky, 13) Pete Rozelle, 14) Martina Navratilova, 15) Henry Aaron, 16) John Wooden, 17) Secretariat, 18) Joe Nameth, 19) Dr. Harold Gores, 20) Jack Nicklaus, 21) Bill Russell, 22) Howard Cosell, 23) Joe Montana, 24) Paul (Bear) Bryant, 25) Roberto Clemente, 26) Olga Korbut, 27) Arthur Ashe, 28) Richard Petty, 29) Bill Rasmussen, 30) Pele, 31) Bobby

Orr, 32) Sugar Ray Leonard, 33) Jim Fixx, 34) Nolan Ryan, 35) Peggy Fleming, 36) Don King, 37) Dr. Robert Jackson, 38) Greg Lemond, 39) Gary Davidson, and 40) Julius Erving.[9]

As of this writing, after 14 years of making music, R.E.M. (which stands for rapid eye movement) is one of the most influential bands on the planet. And leading the charge from this band is 34-year-old Michael Stipe, but again as with sports figures and movie stars, popular singers will change.

Here's a quick look at what *Billboard* magazine, the bible of the music industry, came up with as most popular. Billboard magazine celebrated its 100th anniversary in 1994 and tabulated key all-time hits. The top two in each category are:

Hot 100 (pop single)
"I Will Always Love You" by Whitney Houston
"End of the Road" by Boyz II Men

The Billboard 200 (pop albums)
Thriller by Michael Jackson
My Fair Lady by original cast

Hot Rhythm & Blues Single
"Bump N' Grind" by R. Kelly
"Tossin' and Turnin' " by Bobby Lewis

Top R & B Albums
Thriller by Michael Jackson
Please Hammer Don't Hurt 'Em by M. C. Hammer

Hot Country Singles and Tracks
"Walk On By" by Leroy Van Dyke
"Please Help Me, I'm Falling" by Hank Locklin

Top Country Albums
No Fences by Garth Brooks
Always & Forever by Randy Travis[10]

You might be saying, "I don't know all these sports stars or celebrities," or "None of those celebrities are my child's heroes." That's okay, the most popular celebrities and sports stars change almost weekly. To find out the "biggest" and "hottest" on the sports or music scene or in Hollywood, pick up one of the magazines mentioned or one of the weekly "scandal" papers. Major newspapers and weekly news magazines dedicate a large portion of their space to reporting on these celebrities. Just think: a national newspaper thought that Oprah Winfrey running a marathon in 4 hours, 29 minutes, and 20 seconds was major news! The President of the United States only received one page of coverage for his State of the Union Address, while O. J. Simpson received three pages in *USA Today*! Obviously the public has an ongoing interest in the "rich and famous." People want to know who the current stars are and what they are doing. This is especially evident in gossip papers such as *Enquirer* and the *Star* whose combined circulations exceeds six million!

Take a few minutes now to record who is in the news today.

_____ _____ _____ _____

_____ _____ _____ _____

The fascination over celebrities

Now that we have a feeling for who the celebrities and sports stars are, other questions arise.

- What is so attractive about these idols?
- Why are our youth fascinated by certain contemporary individuals/groups?
- What can parents do about our children idolizing celebrities?

There are a variety of reasons why teens are extremely interested in stars. Fame and fortune top the list—fame meaning glory and celebrity status, and fortune obviously meaning wealth.

Fame means the glitz and glamour, and the incredible attention the stars receive. The media places great emphasis on notoriety. And fame no longer guarantees that a person is known and respected for being a positive role model. Actors, actresses, and politicians receive tremendous amounts of attention for doing something wrong. They receive honorary status for breaking the law or committing obtrusive acts. Parents and teachers become understandably concerned when people become well-known and admired for doing something wrong. Unfortunately the media love this kind of news. It is our responsibility to clarify to our child what these individuals have done. We will discuss this more later on in the chapter.

The most obvious attraction seems to be money. Let's take a quick look at the richest people in the world. Here's how Forbes ranks the rich (not counting royalty and other heads of state), their worth noted in billions:

1. Bill Gates, USA (computers) 9.4
2. Warren Buffett, USA (stock market) 9.2
3. Yoshiaki Tsutsumi, Japan (land) 8.5
4. Carlos Slim Helu, Mexico (conglomerates) 6.6
5. Lee Shau Kee, Hong Kong (land) 6.5
6. John Kluege, USA (media) 5.9
7. (tie) Erivan Haub, Germany (supermarkets) 5.8
     Li Ka-shing, Hong Kong, (land)
8. Emilio Azcarraga Milmo, Mexico (media) 5. 4
9. Kenneth Thomson, Canada (publishing) 5.2
10. Edward Johnson, USA (Fidelity Investments) 5.1[11]

To my knowledge, these individuals, although rich, are not idols of today's youth. So the attraction is not just the money, it is a combination of fame and fortune and also a blend of other factors. Other reasons include attractive appearance, a special skill or talent such as athletic ability or a musical talent, certain admirable innate characteristics and traits, an achievement, and sometimes just being different. Also the admiring child may just be going along with what other kids are interested in, imitating the "in thing." In the final analysis, admiring these qualities is fine, even admiring fame and fortune, if kept in balance.

As parents, we can help our children find that balance. Balance regarding fame and fortune might best be summarized by these sayings: "Success is not so much achievement as achieving"; or "It is nice to be important but it is more important to be nice"; and "It is not money that is evil, but rather the love of money." Let's investigate finding balance in these other factors.

Our society places a major emphasis on beauty. Magazines, commercials, and ads of all types emphasize glamour and being fit and trim as the ultimate goal in life. Attractiveness is displayed nationally and also throughout the towns and communities. When I was the manager of one of the nation's top fitness clubs and part of the club's management team, we fell into this trap. When we worked on newspaper and television ads for the health club, we selected attractive and in-shape models. But eventually we realized we were not depicting real people and in some ways were chasing away those people who needed the health facilities the most. Fortunately, one of the owners was truly interested in getting people fit and not just in having a beauty club or "fit factory." The ads were changed to include member testimonials and photos of people representing all ages and sizes.

My concern is that, for some youth "looking good" like television stars becomes an obsession. For example, if a teen strives for the "perfect" look or weight and becomes anorexic or uses steroids, then the focus on looks is negative. As a parent, display support for and give attention to your child's health and fitness but watch for excessive emphasis by your child on beauty and charm.

Another admiring quality that needs to be kept in balance is your child's infatuation with a special skill or talent such as sports. This quality is a major focus in our society, particularly as noted earlier how sports ranks so high in television viewing. The Super Bowl has become an amazing phenomena and, for many people, all activities other then watching the game stop on that Sunday in January. My son, Ryan, has become part of that group. Ryan wants to be a football player. We have been hearing things like, "I was born to be a football player," and "Football is my life," and "When I'm a wide receiver I want to go by the name Curtis Kraehmer." With his attraction in football, January becomes a month of intense football trivia and interest for him. Before the 1994 Super Bowl with San Francisco and San Diego, he asked who I wanted to win. Realizing San Francisco was an 18 point favorite, I replied "San Diego." Somewhat stunned by my answer, he said, "Why did you pick that team?" I explained, "I like rooting for the underdog. Both teams want to win and it's always exciting to see a 'Cinderella' finish for a team such as this." Ryan nodded, although somewhat confused by my selection.

Knowing that practically Ryan's whole school was picking San Francisco, I continued with my explanation, "Both teams are great, but only one is the greatest in the eyes of the media. Players on both teams worked hard to get to the Super Bowl and should be commended." I pointed out that today's hero usually dwindles into history. I said, "Remember Joe Montana, once designated the best quarterback of the century? His sports card at mall card show was nowhere near as valuable as Steve Youngs, the quarterback of San Francisco." I stopped talking, realizing that my making a point about "winning isn't everything" was bordering on becoming a lecture. "I do think San Francisco will win. I hope it is a close game," I said. I hope he understood my point that although winning is important and worth celebrating, both teams worked very hard to get there and all players should feel good about this major accomplishment.

Many times youth are attracted to celebrities for their achievements. Achievement means different things to different people. A major accomplishment for someone on the celebrity level could mean being on a Wheaties box or winning an Olympic medal, or winning the Stanley Cup or an Academy Award or being part of a touring rock band. Stressing these achievements to your child helps point out the end result but point out to them the process. Achievements are wonderful examples of hard work, perseverance, and goal setting. It is also helpful to examine what positive personality traits the person has to achieve their goal.

What they did or *how* they did it is influential, but more significant is pursuing and investigating a person further for the characteristic or value important to the celebrity—the who they are. Take, for instance, Michael Jordan, who is known for his outstanding performance on the basketball court. Obviously his striking basketball skills are impressive but so are his other qualities. Just as significant as his talent on the court may be his inner strength in dealing with the murder of his father or his determination to pursue another sport, baseball.

Another reason youth are attracted to these icons is just to have different interests from their parents, particularly in music and clothes. This can be seen whenever a new song comes out that kids really like and that they think is their kind of music. If you tell them it is just a remake of one of your favorite songs, what a surprise and a disappointment it is to the child that you know it and like it!

Attraction to certain celebrities also relates to what's *in* with other kids. Remember, peer pressure is powerful. However, interest in certain individuals usually changes quickly.

A helpful hint with all of this: Use these celebrities as topics of discussion concerning health and fitness, ability and talent, aspirations and achievements, personality traits, and uniqueness. Show an interest in the celebrities because it shows an interest in your child.

Now why do youth idolize and envy these icons? I will pose four questions, with responses, to help clarify this quandary. The first question is: Do our youth idolize these icons because the media overglorifies the wealth and power of the stars? To a certain extent, yes, but remember you do have control over your child's environment (reread chapter 5).

A second query is: Are our youth turning more to these idols because they are not finding the needed values, self- and family-esteem, and communication at home? Again yes. That is why it is essential to continually review the five insights.

1. Understand who your child's #1 hero and role model is—YOU!
2. Know and share your values and demonstrate them to your child.
3. Strengthen your child's self-esteem and family-esteem.
4. Talk with your child and, more important, listen.
5. Examine your child's environment, determine what you can do to enhance or if necessary, change it, and teach your child about choices and consequences that relate to your child's well-being.

A third question is: Do our youth want to be different, to be unique in some way, to have their generation look and act a little different? Is this why youth idolize stars and celebrities? This is true to a point, but as a recent *Reader's Digest* poll shows, Americans in every age group share basic values far more than social analysts would have us believe.

Researcher Everett C. Ladd shares this conclusion, "The results (across four generations)—some of the most powerful I have encountered in 30 years of public-opinion research— show that even though young people buy different CDs and clothes, they do not buy into a set of values different from their elders."[12]

Rather, the *Reader's Digest* poll found that, by huge margins:
- Americans young and old still believe this is a land where hard work will be rewarded and dreams can be realized.
- Americans young and old oppose limiting individual opportunity to enforce equality of income.
- Americans young and old increasingly fear the threat of big government.
- Americans young and old believe in God, pray often, and continue the religious heritage that has always marked this nation.[13]

And the fourth question we can ask is: Are our youths searching for themselves via these celebrities and super stars? I would say definitely yes! This is the real why. It comes down to realizing that hero-worshiping is a process for our youth to discover who they want to be. They are dreaming of what their personality should be, what they should look like, how much money they want, what lifestyle to live, and what vocation to pursue. They are trying to find themselves.

This investigation of self usually begins at a young age with cartoons. The heroes of older children are more likely to be real people, or at least human characters from books, television, or the movies. One reason for this shift is that the hero serves different developmental purposes. By identifying with a larger-than-life character, a child can sample how it feels to be brave or romantic, famous or attractive. Heroes offer a youngster an opportunity to sample adolescence while he is a child, and adulthood while he is a teenager.[14]

What can you as a parent do to make this stardom phase (trance? hysteria?) helpful and a worthwhile growth experience?

Parent as a mirror

The focus of chapters 1 through 5 was on your responsibility of parent as hero, being the candle, the flame, the fire. Now I want to make you aware of another role you have regarding heroes—being a mirror. You are to be a mirror that reflects the positive aspects of celebrities—not a lecturer. This should be fun. If you have taken your role as parent as hero seriously and dedicated your time and energy to it, being a mirror becomes interesting and entertaining.

Be honest and sincere in this area. Do not lecture. Your job is to inform, acknowledge, and question. You are *supporting* your child in this area, not "parenting," disciplining, or training.

An example of this mirroring is explaining that TV's Mighty Morphin Power Rangers were banned by a Scandinavian network after a five-year-old Norwegian girl was stoned and kicked by playmates and left to freeze to death. Let your child make a deduction from this. Another example is how the stars of the television show 90201 were not wearing seat belts on the show and how teens watching this were upset. State information like this and let your child make the obvious conclusion.

So what else can you do specifically to mirror celebrities' positive attributes?

Learn about the stars with your child

Read about them in newspapers and magazines. Write letters to the stars. Start a scrap book about them. And realize many times your child's fascination with a certain star is a phase. Our son Ryan went from interest in Ninja Turtles to Power Rangers and now on to football players.

There are plenty of books and magazines about celebrities. There's even a special calendar, "The Dead Celeb Calendar: A Day by Day Look into Their Lives, Accomplishments and Deaths."

Help your child discover the humanness of stars

Point out that along with the fame and fortune, bad things do happen to them. When sports stars get injured or when celebrities get sick, have accidents, get fined, and have family problems, talk over these occurrences with your child. Here are just a few examples:

- Roberto Clemente was killed in a plane crash while bringing relief supplies for victims of a major earthquake in Nicaragua.
- Lou Gehrig became so weak from amyotrophic lateral sclerosis that before his death he was unable to swallow a mouthful of water.
- Harry Chapin was killed instantly while traveling along the Long Island Expressway when an erratic driver, whose license had been suspended several times, slammed into his car.
- Gilda Radner died in her sleep at Cedars-Sinai Hospital in Los Angeles at the age of 42 from ovarian cancer.
- Florence Ballard, one of the Supremes and among the

era's biggest stars, experienced financial difficulties and went on welfare, and two years later died of cardiac arrest.

Make your child aware of
the negatives of stardom

Tell how stardom and politics open up the celebrity's personal life to the whole world. Show how the media announces all of the personal activities of famous people. Talk about how this puts tremendous pressure on the celebrity as do other aspects of being famous.

Discuss with your child how prestige and stardom can be easily lost or taken away if the pressure is too great and how deterioration takes place whether it be from alcohol, drugs, violence, or flamboyant spending. Just a few of the many examples include:

- The 32-year-old singer Karen Carpenter died of a heart attack brought on by anorexia nervosa.
- John Bonham, drummer for the rock group Led Zeppelin, was found dead in the palatial home of the group's lead guitarist, Jimmy Page. According to the coroner's report, John "Bonzo" Bonham died from asphyxiation caused by vomiting after drinking an estimated 40 shots of vodka over a 12-hour period.
- In December, 1980, when John and Yoko Lennon were returning to their home from a recording studio, an emotionally unstable fan, Mark David Chapmann, fired five shots at John Lennon's back. Lennon died shortly afterwards at the hospital.
- George Reeves, who played the original Superman on television for six years, killed himself.
- The life of talented young actor River Phoenix ended outside a trendy Sunset Strip bar owned by his pal Johnny Depp. The 23-year-old collapsed on the sidewalk. An autopsy revealed cocaine, heroin, traces of marijuana, and Valium were in his body.
- Ty Cobb, a legendary athlete, set a record for career

runs scored (2,245) and a lifetime batting average (.367) that have endured over 65 years since he retired, but he was also an abusive, racist, and self-serving individual.

Emphasize that money is not everything

As adults we eventually learn that money buys many things but not usually peace and contentment. No doubt money is necessary but financial contentment means realizing that it is not money that is evil but rather the love of money. Discuss the principles surrounding money and its power with your child. An organization entitled Ministry of Money offers a helpful description of money that may be a good starting point for a dialogue on this topic:

"Money is one of the most powerful forces in each of our lives; for some of us, it is the main force. In our society, money represents power, pleasure, security and status. But money also brings fear, guilt, insecurity, greed and selfishness. We've all been haunted by most of these feelings. Money is a paradox—it enslaves, yet it also frees; it is intensely private, but it is very public; it measures worth, yet it is no measure of real worth; it destroys but also creates."[15]

Here's some additional food for thought on the topic of money.

In 1923, a very important meeting was held at the Edgewater Beach Hotel in Chicago. Attending this meeting were eight of the world's most successful financiers. Those present were:

The president of the largest independent steel company;
The president of the largest gas company;
The greatest wheat speculator;
The president of the New York Stock Exchange;
A member of the President's cabinet;
The greatest "bear" in Wall Street;

Head of the world's greatest monopoly;
The president of the Bank of International Settlements.

Certainly we must admit that here were gathered a group of the world's most successful men—at least, men who had found the secret of "making money."

Let's see what happened to these men 25 years later.
The president of the largest steel company—Charles Schwab—died a bankrupt man and lived on borrowed money for five years before his death.
The president of the largest gas company—Howard Hopson—was then insane.
The greatest wheat speculator—Arthur Cutten—died abroad, insolvent.
The president of the New York Stock Exchange—Richard Whitney—had been released from Sing Sing penitentiary.
The member of the President's cabinet—Albert Fall—was pardoned from prison so he could die at home.
The greatest "bear" in Wall Street—Jesse Livermore—committed suicide.
The world's greatest Match King, head of the International Financial Agency—Ivan Kreuger—committed suicide.
The president of the Bank of International Settlements—Leon Fraser—committed suicide.
All these men learned well the art of making money, but not one of them learned how to live!

Many times a parent's discussion on money can border on becoming a lecture, but our children need to discover these truths on their own. It is not an easy lesson to learn. Your strategy in talking about money is to make it a two-way discussion. Reflect the idea that it is not what you have but who you are. The what, "the things," will come. The point to make is that wealthy celebrities and sports stars have a skill, a talent, a gift that they achieved through training and perseverance. They have developed from the inside out; financial success is a by-product of sharing their talent.

Point out positive aspects of stars and athletes

Celebrities have talents, skills, and have made accomplishments and contribution to a team, society, and history. Read, watch shows, and talk about people such as Colonel Sanders, Malcolm X, Jim Hensen, Martin Luther King, Christy McAuliffe, Jackie Onassis, Dr. Seuss, or Henry Fonda with your child.

Besides these renowned deceased individuals, it is essential to discuss contemporary stars. My son Ryan made me aware of this point while riding in the car listening to the radio. Many of the radio stations were playing Elvis Presley songs. One announcer made the statement, "It would have been Elvis' 60th birthday today." Ryan, somewhat irritated by what was said, complained, "What's the big deal about what he would have been, he's dead!"

And my son's statement is true regarding admiration of celebrities by our children. Although many celebrities gain legendary status after they die, your child is focusing on individuals that are significant today. And every day many positive figures emerge.

There was an ad in the paper by HandsNet's Youth Development Forum which use a play on words to emphasize there are positive "icons." It read:

"Proof that Beavis and Butthead aren't the only icons for American youth today."

The point is well taken and here's just a few of positive role models and high achievers:

- Tiger Woods, 18, of Cypress, California staged the greatest comeback in the 99-year history of U. S. Amateur gold championship to become the tournament's youngest champion. He is quoted as saying, "The only time I felt like I won was when I hugged my father."
- Dr. Marion Tinsley played a 30-game match at the World Checkers Championship in Boston against Chinook, a supercomputer.
- 1994 U. S. A. speed skater Dan Jansen won the gold

medal in a record-breaking time after being denied the gold medal in three straight Olympic games.

- Bonnie Blair competed in four consecutive Olympics and collected five gold medals and a bronze.
- Amy Grant, pop singer, earned five platinum and three gold records as well as numerous Grammy and Dove awards.
- Brazilian goalkeeper Claudio Taffarel made saves during the shootout at the end of the 1994 WorldCup championship game against Italy.
- Dave Dravecky, the former major league baseball player who lost his all-star pitching arm to cancer in 1991, founded the Dave Dravecky Foundation to help people live courageously.
- Dave Thomas, founder of Wendy's restaurants, got a high school diploma 45 years after dropping out of school.
- Miami Dolphins tight end, Keith Jackson, raised over three million dollars for a sports and education facility he is building in East Little Rock for 400 disadvantaged youths in grades 8-11.
- Mary Lou Retton was an Olympic gymnast and the first woman on the cover of a Wheaties box.
- Cathy Rigby was probably the best all-around Olympic gymnast the United States ever produced up until the 1972 Olympics and is now a star of the musical theater.
- Alabamian Heather Whitestone who was told as a child by doctors that she would never go beyond the third grade, became the 1995 Miss America.

And there are many other celebrity-type individuals beyond the Super Bowl stars, Olympic athletes, and winners of Academy and Emmy Awards. Many other distinguished individuals are pursuing their dreams, making noted accomplishments, and finding their place in history. These include Nobel Prize, Pulitzer Prize, and Spingarn Medal winners. Become aware of candidates and selected winners for these prestigious awards.

Nobel Prize. Alfred B. Nobel (1833-1896), inventor of dynamite, bequeathed $9,000,000, the interest to be distributed yearly to those who had most benefited humankind in physics, chemistry, medicine-physiology, literature, and peace. Prizes in these five areas were first awarded in 1901. The first Nobel Memorial Prize in Economic Science was awarded in 1969, funded by the central bank of Sweden.

Pulitzer Prize. The Pulitzer Prizes in Journalism, Letters, and Music were endowed by Joseph Pulitzer (1847-1911), publisher of the *New York World*, in a bequest to Columbia University and are awarded annually by the president of the university on recommendation of the Pulitzer Prize Board for work done during the preceding year.

Spingarn Medal. The Spingarn Medal has been awarded annually since 1914 by the National Association for the Advancement of Colored People (NAACP) for the highest achievement by a black American.

Nominees for these awards are well-known in the areas of education and research and can be a catalyst for your child to uncover what he or she wants to be or accomplish. These individuals and their accomplishments offer excellent models for your child's dreams and ambitions.

Whether the goal be acting, music, sports, or education, let your child dream. Help your child see the greatness of these people and also their humanness. Help your child be motivated by the positive traits and achievements of these icons. Aid your child in seeing the distinction between stars and heroes. Make a concerted effort to reflect the positive aspects of celebrities and sports stars. Also talk about past idols and what happened to them.

Take time to listen to what your child is expressing about these celebrities. Learn from what your child is saying and notice the ways in which your child explores his or her feelings and relates your child's own situations through these celebrities. Be aware when your child becomes obsessed with a particular person. This may signal your child's need for attention, clarification, or support. He or she may be troubled. If a parent has been neglectful regarding the five insights, whether intentionally or not, a child begins to look toward celebrities and super stars as heroes and sees fame, fortune, and being number one as the ultimate goal. Be patient. Be caring. Continue building your child's self-esteem.

One final point is that it is possible for a Hollywood star or sports figure to become an authentic hero. It happens when the celebrity reaches out and performs a deed that provides a meaningful, positive change in someone. The hero status is then bestowed on this celebrity by the person who is inwardly changed by something the celebrity did. There are many actors and actresses doing these deeds.

Individuals such as these were recognized as *USA Weekend's* 1995 Most Caring Athletes. Included were Chris Zorich from the Chicago Bears, Kirby Puckett from the Minnesota Twins, and Adam Graves from the New York Rangers. One winner, Kevin Johnson from the Phoenix Suns, who opened St. Hope Academy in Sacramento, California, says "I take my role model status very seriously." The facility is a home for 48 boys and girls where they can study, play, and most important, feel at home. Another winner, tennis pro Michael Chang, organized the Tennis Stars of the Future program in Hong Kong, which provides children from the poorest sections of Hong Kong with tennis equipment and coaching. He states "If I'm able to influence kids in a positive way, get them on the right track and away from some of the things that might hurt them—whether it's being involved with the wrong kids or being involved with drugs or alcohol—I feel that's part of my job."

These celebrities as heroes are well-known masters in their field of movies or athletics, but they are also quiet heroes helping others. In closing this chapter, I would like to share a story from the movie, *Rudy*, that touched and inspired my family.

Daniel E. Ruettiger was probably known in the Chicago area back in 1975 but it was not until 1995, when the movie about him came out, that the nation learned about him.

Daniel, known to his family and friends as "Rudy," grew up admiring the University of Notre Dame football team on television. And Rudy had a dream. One evening in his living room he told his parents he would someday play football for Notre Dame. His family laughed.

After playing high school football and graduating, he worked in a steel mill, but his dream was kept alive by a supporting friend. After the tragic death of his friend, Rudy took action toward his dream. His first hurdle was acceptance into Notre Dame University; he also had to compensate for his small size when trying out for the team.

Rudy eventually attended Notre Dame and tried out for the football team. He ended up on the practice team and practiced hard. He became known for his persistence and enthusiasm. Rudy's reward was an overwhelming respect from his teammates and an opportunity to dress for the last home game against Georgia Tech and go out the "tunnel."

The inspiring take-away from the movie was the value of having a dream and pursuing it and thus gaining respect from his teammates. But the principal message was the idea that it is not what you have that counts but who you become and what effect you have on others. Rudy is an example of a positive role model, and most likely he was a hero to many of his teammates.

Hollywood stars, professional athletes, and even educational geniuses, for the most part, are the idols of today, not genuine heroes. But they do provide inspiration, entertainment, and a fantasy world for youth. We should understand that our children will envy certain individuals and groups and realize that that's okay—it is part of growing up. This admiration is really good as long as it does not cause negative "copycat" behavior in your child.

Your job as parent is to assist your child in keeping these icons in perspective but yet to allow your child to have his or her own celebrity models. Just continue your role as hero, and allow celebrities to become the lesser icons.

Though fame is smoke, its fumes are frankincense to human thoughts.
    —George Byron (1788-1824)
    English Poet

7

Heroes or Famous Personalities?

Mythological Characters and Historical Figures

If you create an act, you create a habit.
If you create a habit, you create a character.
If you create a character, you create a destiny.
    —Andre Maurois (1885- 1967)
        French Author

Franklin Delano Roosevelt helped millions of people as President of the United States for thirteen years. He took office in 1933 when more than 13 million people were unemployed, many farmers and city workers were homeless, and thousands of banks were closing daily. To many people during the 1930's, Franklin Roosevelt was a hero.

Any number of politicians look up to Roosevelt as a role model. Bill Clinton and Newt Gingrich have publicly admired Roosevelt's ability in leading the nation through two major crises, a severe depression, and a global war.

Here in the Hudson Valley thousands of tourists visit Roosevelt's home in Hyde Park. Just last summer our family visited the Roosevelt estate. I, too, was impressed by his leadership. Like Clinton and Gingrich, I admire Roosevelt for guiding a nation during a very difficult time and also for his courage and determination to conquer infantile paralysis. And as we toured his home and museum, my sons found Roosevelt fascinating because they saw a picture of him with a fish he caught that was as large as a person!

This demonstrates the many levels of admiration for historical figures. Some people classify as heroes certain well-known figures from the history books—political, religious, and war-time leaders. If we refer back to my definition of hero, which is "a hero performs a deed that provides a meaningful, positive change in someone," some were truly heroes in their time while most are now classified as famous personalities that are well-respected.

Obviously many of these leaders have assisted a significant number of people, but their actions were in the past and are not making a direct change in someone today. The key words here are "direct" and "today." Semantics? I don't think so. Remember we are discussing our children's heroes. For our children, a deed that provides a meaningful, positive change means having some type of personal contact with an individual and experiencing a direct influence. Hearing or reading about these famous historic figures is indirect and removed. Therefore, these individuals are not heroes to your child, but most likely were heroes to others in the past.

And how about mythological characters? Why do I associate these with historical figures in this chapter? Partly because of the heroic nature of these characters and the wide respect they have been given over the years. But the main reason for including myths with history is that as time passes these two sometimes become one.

The chopping down of the cherry tree by George Washington is surely the most famous truth-telling tale in America, but was it real or fiction? Stories told by Holocaust survivors may seem like myths to your child and only become "real" to your child when he or she sees pictures or visits the Holocaust Museum in Washington, D.C. Another example is the sinking of the Titanic. Melissa Peltier, producer of a four-hour examination of this disaster, says, "It's almost like a Greek myth that really happened in our lifetime." She explains, "It's so unbelievable. It's so mythic. The little human stories on board. All the morality plays that are happening, just the whole idea of the arrogance and the hubris of speeding through the ice field because (they thought) nothing could go wrong. It's a huge moral lesson."[1]

There are literally hundreds of examples that illustrate the confusion of historical facts and tales. The point is that, despite the confusion regarding historical figures and mythological characters, they are both important. And for the most part, to your child, neither group represents heroes. These individuals are just interesting and admirable characters.

Keep in mind two points: 1) Historical figures are heroes to some people, but, for the most part, they are usually impressive individuals who have shown great character or performed major accomplishments;

2) There is a definite similarity between history and mythology. Both include respected (and despicable) characters, and there are lessons to be learned from both types.

Let us take a brief look at some historical and mythological characters who are respected. Then I will give pointers on how to help your child become interested in history and mythology and how these characters can be helpful in your child's development.

A few recently famous people include Geraldine Ferraro, the first major-party female vice-presidential candidate in U.S. history; Terry Anderson, the former chief Middle East Correspondent for the Associated Press who was held hostage by Shiite fundamentalists in Lebanon for over six years; Nelson Mandela, the Nobel-Prize-winning president of South Africa; and Mother Teresa, possibly the woman most caring of the poor in the world.

Famous American historical figures are many. Here are just a few: Abraham Lincoln, Henry Ford, Thomas Jefferson, Benjamin Franklin, Clara Barton, Helen Keller, Dr. Elizabeth Blackwell, Harriet Tubman, and Martin Luther King, Jr. Some of Canada's famous people include Alexander Mackenzie (1789 Arctic voyage), Joseph Boyle (struck it rich during the Klondike Gold Rush), Nova Scotia mariner Joshua Slocum (first person to sail alone around the globe), Wop May and his fellow aviators pushing back the boundaries of Canada's last frontier, Marc Garneau and Roberts Bondar (aviators), one-legged Terry Fox (raised money for cancer research), activist

Nellie McClung, Saskatchewan's Tommy Douglas (social activist and the father of socialized medicine), Laura Secord (warned the British of an American attack), and Red Cross nurse Elisabeth Carrier.

Each year in New York City's Radio City Music Hall, hundreds of thousands of people are reminded of a historical figure of long ago. On stage and in the show's program, the life of this man is described. This individual had, and still has, a significant effect on the world. This man has been described in this way:

He was born in an obscure village, the child of a peasant woman. He grew up in another obscure village, where He worked in a carpenter shop until He was thirty. Then for three years He was an itinerant preacher. He never had a family or owned a home. He never set foot inside a big city. He never traveled two hundred miles from the place He was born. He never wrote a book or held an office. He did none of the things that usually accompany greatness.

While He was still a young man, the tide of popular opinion turned against Him. His friends deserted Him. He was turned over to His enemies and went through the mockery of a trial. He was nailed to a cross between two thieves. While He was dying, His executioners gambled for the only piece of property He had—His coat. When He was dead He was taken down and laid in a borrowed grave.

Nineteen centuries have come and gone, and today He is the central figure for much of the human race. All the armies that ever marched, and all the navies that ever sailed, and all the parliaments that ever sat, and all the kings that ever reigned, put together have not affected the life of man upon this earth as powerfully as this "One Solitary Life"—the life of Jesus Christ.

There are many individuals from biblical times, such as Adam and Eve, Cain and Abel, and Moses, who some may classify as myths. Christianity is by no means the only religion with such figures. All religions have people who are significant to their culture, history, and religious doctrine—some historical, some mythological.

Most cultures include a hierarchy of divine creatures or gods that they worship and supplicate. Filling the gap between the gods are the superheroes of myth and legend. In them we create god-like creatures out of our dreams and ambitions. We see ourselves enlarged—a vision of what we could be were we not limited by our weaknesses. Because our mythical heroes are both human and superhuman, they provide us with an ideal that is within our grasp, not completely impossible and unrealistic.[2]

While Western culture relies primarily on rational and historical modes of interpretation and understanding, the study of myth remains one of the fruitful approaches that aids in the understanding of human reality.

Some of more well-known Western myths include Mesopotamian, Egyptian, Canaanite, Indian, Roman, Norse (Germanic and Scandinavian), Celtic, and the best known Greek myths. Many people are familiar with the famous Greek tale about King Midas and his lust for gold; the myth of Narcissus whose vanity and heartlessness have made his name forever synonymous with intense self-infatuation; the tale about Perseus battling the fearful Medusa, whose hair is snakes, whose glance turns men to stone; the myth of Theseus facing the Minotaur—half man, half bull, without armor, without weapons; the story of Daedalus and Icarus determined to thwart the gods with Icarus flying too near the sun; the tale of the beautiful, hard-hearted, swift-footed Atalanta meeting her match in a lover who understands feminine curiosity; and the myth of Pygmalion and Galatea in which a young sculptor carves the world's most beautiful statue and falls in love with it.

Asian and African cultures have wonderful folk tales, and most of us are familiar with American fables such as Three Little Kittens, Jack and the Beanstalk, Little Steam Engine, Mike Mulligan and His Steam Shovel, and Chicken Little that have survived generations of story-telling.

History, myths, and fables are wonderful avenues for visualizing certain positive characteristics, achievements, and lessons to be learned. Although adolescents may not be openly interested in these subjects, the following activity may be a start and could spark an interest. Here's a little quiz for you and your child to take. See how many of these characters are real and which are fictional. You should do it first and then let your child take the challenge. When you go to check your answers (sorry no answers given—spend some time researching them with your child), it will be a fun and educational experience.

Anne Sullivan	Pocahontas
Robinson Crusoe	Sybil Ludington
Hero of Alexandria	David and Goliath
Paul Revere	Plato
Hans Christian Anderson	Tom Sawyer
Robert Scott	Shakespeare
Buffalo Bill	Willie Wonka
Strega Nona	Henry Kissinger
Sitting Bull	Peter The Great
Christy	Sherlock Holmes
Alfred Hitchcock	Henry VIII
Hunchback of Notre Dame	Ms. Frizzle
Frank Lloyd Wright	Hero and Leander
Saint Augustine	Joseph Campbell
Lewis and Clark	Nathan Hale

How did you do? History and mythology offers a lot of interesting people and characters to investigate. So what do you do to spark an interest in these admirable figures and how can this help your child grow?

First enjoy this subject of history and myth—don't make it a chore for you or your child. It might take a little research on your part to find some interesting facts about certain characters, but do have fun with it.

Also read and tell stories. Here's just a sampling of what is available.

There is *A History of the World in the Twentieth Century* by J. A. S. Grenville; *The Young Reader's Companion to American History*, 964 pages of history by more than 150 historians, Pulitzer Prize winners and Newbery Medalists; and *The Timetables of African American History* by Sharon Harley. Young adults might be interested in a series entitled *The Importance of* . . . . Each volume keys in on an individual who has made a unique contribution to history in the areas of politics, music, art, literature, philosophy, science, sports, or religion. Included in this series are individuals such as Cleopatra, Christopher Columbus, Marie Curie, Thomas Edison, Albert Einstein, Galileo Galilei, Chief Joseph, Malcolm X, Margaret Mead, Michelangelo, Wolfgang Amadeus Mozart, Napoleon Bonaparte, Richard M. Nixon, Jackie Robinson, Anwar Sadat, Margaret Sanger, Mark Twain, and H. G. Wells. You can also find stories on CD-ROM such as *The Cartoon History of the Universe*.

The Fables of Aesop are timeless and well-known. The interest in fables has been growing since the recent publication of *Fables* by Arnold Lobel. Also, *The Complete Fairy Tales of the Brothers Grimm and Goddesses, Heroes, and Shaman* are popular with children ages 10 and up.

Another positive way for you to introduce history and mythology to your child is through television programs. Unfortunately, history is not usually appreciated until adulthood. Fortunately, Hollywood has offered some assistance to make it appealing to the younger generation.

Libraries and video stores offer many movies and documentaries on famous individuals. For example a four-part video on the Titanic is available.

One of my all-time favorite videos is "The Three Little Pigs" by Faerie Tale Theatre. The theme is much like the original story, but the dialogue and acting have been enhanced, and humor has been added. The live cast acting and story line are absolutely delightful and entertaining. Billy Crystal is the pig who builds the brick house, Jeff Goldblum is the wolf, Valerie Perrine is a female swine, and Doris Roberts is the three pigs' mother. Ryan and Zachary know I love this story and they watch it with me every time. Its wonderful lesson is obvious—the importance of doing a job right. CBS Fox Video has re-created many wonderful tales into shows where actors and actresses perform these fairy tales. Some of these include *Cinderella, Sleeping Beauty, Pinocchio, Hansel and Gretel, Aladdin and His Wonderful Lamp, The Nightingale, The Frog Prince,* and *Puss 'N Boots.* The exciting part about these tales is that they are stories for all ages, including teenagers, to enjoy. Check them out—you will not be disappointed.

A third way to create an attraction to historical and mythological characters is by visiting historic sights and looking for representations of famous and also not-so-famous people.

For example, Charles Lindbergh is well-known for the first solo, non-stop flight across the Atlantic on May 21, 1927 in The Spirit of St. Louis. But if one researches more on Lindbergh, you will find out that his son was kidnapped and murdered which led to a federal law on kidnapping, popularly know as the Lindbergh Act. Further research will also reveal that Charles Lindbergh won a Pulitzer Prize for his autobiography, *The Spirit of Saint Louis* in 1953.

The importance of introducing historical people to your child is for your child to learn about their characteristics and also about history and its significance. Whether it be celebrating Martin Luther King's birthday, Independence Day, or even Valentine's Day, each special event gives you and your child the opportunity to talk about famous people and characters.

Regarding myths and fables, having your child become interested in these tales is an excellent approach to learning lessons and morals. At my place of employment, no one wanted to go against what upper management was suggesting even though it was obvious to many that what management wanted would be harmful to the company. This situation was appropriately compared to the tale of The Emperor's New Clothes, a story in which nobody wanted to tell the king that he had no clothes on. The point is that the messages from these tales and myths are timeless and relate to everyday life situations.

In both categories of famous characters, your child can see

certain human characteristics or traits as examples to follow (if they are positive) or avoid if they are negative. Take time for you and your child to learn about these wonderful historic people and mythological characters. Studying these individuals of the past is entertaining, but having your child grow and change from investigating them is the ultimate goal. A friend shared the following fable which points out the importance of action, not just talk.

This story is a parable—*The Tale of Two Knights* by Karen Burton Mains.

Sir Percival the Promising and Sir Chauncy the Cautious heard tales of battling Woeful Evil from the Chief Minister of the Great King. He had explained the terrible tactics of the Great King's enemy and the danger of dragons and temptation. Both knights agreed, "This Cause is greater than all other causes. I will follow after the Great King." They bellowed in unison, "Hail to the Great King!" and agreed to journey together. And they spurred their horses down the road, shouting, "After we go!"

For many years they traveled thus. Sometimes the going was good, and sometimes—when it rained—it was not.

Whenever possible they turned out of their way to attend a Council of Knights to get inspired by stories of great battles and awesome facts.

Whenever they left one of these Councils, Sirs Percival and Chauncy talked and dreamed of how they would fight for the Cause one day. They talked of facing dragons and enemy armies off the field of battle.

Every day they would spring to their horses and ride until nightfall. But alas, they never seemed to find the service they sought.

Finally the day of the Grand Awards came, and the two

now elderly knights rode to the castle of the Great King to collect what they had won.

"Have ye any scars, any wounds? Did ye meet the flaming one with drawn sword? On what fields of war stood ye? What have ye done for the Great King?" inquired the Great King's Chief Keeper of Accounts.

They thought and thought. And they had to admit they had never carried out one plan.

So the Chief Keeper told them, "No rewards for you. Nothing."

They had mistaken words for action, other peoples' tales for their own. Perhaps you've seen travelers like them on the road of life.

Here's a somewhat humorous true story of a child learning about a historical event and then taking action in his life. Kacey Lange did more than just read about an event in the 1800's, he was changed by it.

A valuable discovery in the 1860's was the discovery of chewing gum. It was discovered by a military general, Antonio Lo'pez de Santa Anna, the despised Mexican commander responsible for the massacre at the Alamo. He brought the tasteless resin to Staten Island, New York. Important individual? For fifth-grader Kacey Lange in Wilmot Elementary School, yes. Besides doing some historical research, Kacey created a journal relating to gum including the results of a project that tested what brand of gum would last the longest amount of time. He was honored with a third place ribbon at his school science fair. He had fun with this topic and also learned something. Of course what Kacey probably found out was that what we buy today is not General Santa Anna's original taffy-like chicle, but a gentler synthetic polymer—polyvinyl acetate—itself tasteless, odorless, and unappetizingly named, which Americans chew at the rate of 10 million pounds per year.[3]

Getting to know about historical and mythological characters is a way for your child to see examples and get ideas. Focus on the example and then help your child focus on the character's important traits and characteristics, whether it be honesty (George Washington), courage (Starbuck of *Moby Dick*), hard work (Booker T. Washington), compassion (Belle of *Beauty and the Beast*), inquisitiveness (Thomas Edison) discipline and self-control (Gandhi), or kindness (the mouse in Aesop's *The Lion and The Mouse*).

Let's summarize what you can do with this topic of historical and mythological characters. Expose your child to these individuals through books, videos, games, and story telling. Be the mirror of these characters. Discuss historical people and mythological characters, but be aware that your viewpoint of a famous person may differ from your child's. For instance, take the three little pigs story. You might think it's obvious who the villain is—the wolf, right? Maybe not. There is a book, *The True Story of the 3 Little Pigs!* by Jon Scieszka, that takes the side of the wolf. His tale starts with a birthday cake for the wolf's dear old granny, a bad head cold, and a bad reputation. Scieszka tries to show how the destruction of the straw and stick houses were accidents—the Wolf was framed. It is a whole new way to look at the pigs and wolf. My point is to remember that just as celebrities, famous people and characters interest our children for different reasons—admiring certain historical and mythological characters is a result of each person's perception. Understand this concept and continue to bring these characters to your child's attention.

Dr. William Pollack, a psychologist at Harvard Medical School, gives this advice on differences of opinions about heroes: "If you're concerned by your child's choice of a hero, don't just try to take it away. Instead, build on your child's choice by introducing him or her to stories about other heroic people and characters who have different values."[4]

It's okay if your child admires famous individuals and mythological characters. Assist him or her in this area, but most of all remember to notice and admire these traits and accomplishments in your child. Compliment your child on his or her positive characteristic or accomplishment. More than just talking about these characteristics in people from history books, nurture and promote these qualities in your child— bring them out in splendid glory. By recognizing your child's potential, these traits will surface and expand. You will strengthen that heroic bond between you and your child. You will be contributing to a big Cause—confidence, self-esteem and the development of a unique person—your child.

Reputation is only a . . . candle, of wavering and uncertain flame, and easily blown out, but it is the light by which the world looks for and finds merit.
—James Lowell (1819-1891)
American Editor, Diplomat

8

Heroes or Angels?

Humanitarians, Good Samaritans, and Courageous Individuals

Without heroes, we are all plain people and don't know how far we can go.
—Bernard Malamud (1914–986)
American Author

Anthony is a friend who owns an auto repair shop just a mile from our home. Our kids go to the same school as his two children, and he repairs our cars. But what I didn't know until just recently was that he is a hero.

A man was trapped under a pickup truck when the vehicle slipped off a pair of lifts. Joseph Rubino and his uncle, Robert Watson, were working underneath the truck when it fell.

Watson was able to wiggle free and was uninjured. But Rubino, who was lying on his side, became pinned beneath the truck's transmission.

Anthony Pisciotta, our friend who owns the Wallkill Service Center and a tow truck operator, was listening to his police band radio at home when he heard that someone was pinned under a truck.

"I jumped in the tow truck. Someone had to get him out from under there," said Pisciotta, who often responds to fire and ambulance calls such as car rollovers and other accidents when he and his truck may be needed.

Pisciotta lives near the scene where Rubino was trapped and got there within minutes. Watson and passers-by were trying to elevate the truck with a street jack. But they were unable

179

to lift it high enough to free Rubino. "He wasn't talking, but he was conscious," Pisciotta said.

Pisciotta chained the pickup to his tow truck, then slowly and carefully lifted it off of the injured man. Rubino was taken to the hospital.

Pisciotta "responded really quickly," said State Police Trooper Diana Benoit, who was also at the scene. "He was definitely the hero of the day."[1]

At an awards banquet later in Baltimore, Maryland, Anthony received a plaque with the following inscription:

The Towman Commendation Courageous Professionalism
in the Endeavor To Save A Human Life
Anthony Pisciotta, Baltimore, Maryland, October 29, 1994
Presented by American Towman Magazine
and Emergency Road Service, Inc.

Anthony is just one of thousands of "people helping people" in emergency agencies, service organizations, and other non-profit and religious organizations. Are these people heroes? In emergency situations such as the above, most definitely. And regarding other people who perform kind and courteous acts, yes again, if the person "performs a deed that provides a meaningful, positive change in someone." These individuals represent a special type of hero, the quiet or unsung hero. They are humanitarians, Good Samaritans and courageous people.

Good Samaritans and other humanitarians make the world a better place. Some people who help others out of kindness and concern eventually become famous. They all started out by wanting to help others on a one-to-one basis. Mother Teresa has dedicated most of her life to helping the poorest of the poor in the slums of India. Dr. Thomas Dooley labored in the jungles of Southeast Asia, bringing medical help to remote villages. Eleanor Roosevelt worked for rights of women and people of color, and Martin Luther King, Jr. led nonviolent civil rights demonstrations. Clara Barton, a founder of the American Association of the Red Cross, tried to bring humanity to the battlefield. George C. Marshall promoted peace through the European Recovery Program. The list of famous and not-so-famous Good Samaritans and humanitarians is endless— Albert Schweitzer, Florence Nightingale, Harriet Tubman, Peace Corps workers, missionaries, substance abuse counselors, hospice workers, ministers, social workers, scout leaders, and all those who have built careers around their concern for others.[2]

In this chapter I would like to share with you many examples of humanitarians, Good Samaritans, and courageous people. My goal is to make you aware of their prominence in today's society, in other words, I want to point out that there still are a lot of caring people out there. They are wonderful examples and role models for your child; take the time to search them out and mirror their specialness. And most likely there will be one or two individuals in this category who touch your child's life personally by their heroic deeds.

Who are some examples of these individuals today? President Clinton has recognized several of them.

In one quick moment, tourists Harry Rakosky and Ken Davis had a choice to make; they could be horrified tourists— or heroes. On Saturday, October 29, 1994, they chose gallantry.

A gunman had just fired bursts at the White House from his Chinese semiautomatic and was fumbling with the gun, possibly trying to reload as tourists fled.

Adrenaline surged through Rakosky, a security specialist, and Davis, a corrections officer in training, as they hurled themselves toward the gunman.

Davis and Rakosky said they did not feel like heroes, yet President Clinton paid tribute to them at a dinner the following Saturday night.

"The man was captured in part because ordinary citizens who were standing there did their duty, and I hope that is an example for others around the country," the President said.[3]

During his second year in office, President Clinton awarded the nation's highest civilian honor, the Medal of Freedom, to nine Americans. The recipients were House Minority Leader Bob Michel; Washington Post cartoonist Herbert Block, better known by his pen name, Herblock; the late Cesar Chavez, founder of the United Farm Workers of America; Arthur Flemming, who served under every president from Franklin Roosevelt to Ronald Reagan, including a stint as Secretary of Health, Education and Welfare; James Grant, executive director of UNICEF; Dorothy Height, a pioneer in civil rights and the National Council of Negro Women; Barbara Jordan, a civil rights champion and former congresswoman; Lane Kirkland, president of the AFL-CIO; and Robert Sargent Shriver, who helped establish the Peace Corps.

There are a variety of recognition programs throughout the year honoring people for their acts of kindness, courage, and assistance.

For the dedication of Public Service Recognition Week in May, 1994, our nation's vice president wrote this open letter to all Americans:

> As Public Service Recognition Week opens, I would like to salute the good people who have devoted their lives to making this nation succeed.
>
> During this week, many of the government's unsung heroes will be recognized in various award ceremonies across the country.
>
> The test of a true democratic society is the degree to which its citizens participate.
>
> Sincerely,
> Al Gore[4]

Parade, the Sunday newspaper magazine, and the International Association of Chiefs of Police (IACP) annually recognize the achievements of the nation's 604,000 police officers and select the Police Officer of the Year Award.

Reader's Digest has a regular feature in the magazine called "Heroes for Today," stories about individuals who have demonstrated courage, kindness, and decency.

Three people were recently recognized for courage by *Reader's Digest*. Scott Robeson, a New York City building superintendent, prevented someone from being robbed at an ATM lobby. After the robber was arrested, Robeson was the center of attention at Carmichael's restaurant near the bank. "He's our local hero," said the bartender. Asked if he would do it again, Robeson said, "Absolutely."

Deborah Dempsey, captain of the transport ship *Lyra*, and her crew received the Admiralty of the Ocean Sea award, the highest recognition in the merchant marine, for saving the *Lyra*. Dempsey and four volunteer crew members prevented an ecological disaster and the loss of the $22-million vessel.

Betsy Hall, 35, was painting her bedroom when she heard heart-rending screams. Two Rottweilers were attacking 10-year-old Kimberly Schreyer after school in Mount Laurel, N.J. The four-foot-eleven, 115-pound housewife picked up a tree limb and started hitting the 100-pound Rottweilers. Then Hall managed to drag Kimberly away from the dogs to safety. Kimberly was flown by helicopter to a hospital and has recovered from the attack.[5]

Maxwell House Coffee's "Real Heroes" program honors Americans who volunteer to fill a need in their communities. The program celebrates Americans who make selfless contributions and personal sacrifices to better their community and other people's lives.

Examples of winners range from ages 11 to 91 and champion a wide array of concerns including homelessness, poverty, AIDS, health care, and services for mentally and physically challenged people. One "Real Hero" climbs Mt. Killimanjaro for charity; another is a wheelchair-bound Emergency Medical Technician; a third has raised 186 foster children; and a fourth serves Thanksgiving dinner to more than 30,000 people each year.

America's Awards is a program of the Positive Thinking Foundation "Honoring Unsung Heroes Who Personify the American Character and Spirit." Criteria for this award specify that the person must be:

1. alive, or have died no more than two years before the nomination is submitted;
2. a U.S. citizen at the time the award is presented;
3. a personification of one specific value that is an important trait of the American character or spirit;
4. capable of inspiring millions of Americans to emulate the value he or she embodies;
5. relatively unknown;
6. of good character.

Recent winners include:

- Abe Brown, Tampa, Fla. for: Dedication
- Stan Curtis, Louisville, Ky. for: Enthusiasm
- Melody Jones, San Antonio, Tex. for: Purpose
- Mike McGarven, Fresno, Calif. for: Sacrifice
- Anne Sweeney, Woodinville, Wash. for: Resourcefulness
- Allan Tibbels, Baltimore, Md. for: Tenacity[6]

And stretching the concept of heroes and kindness, *USA Today* asked readers about the unsung heroes of the travel industry who do a little—or a lot—to make you feel at home when you're away from home. They printed a few of the stories to say thanks to six million U.S. travel industry workers.

I would like to share just a few examples of the tremendous outreach one person can have.

• Jimmy Hogarth from Orkney, Scotland, is a live "scarecrow." The Scottish Natural Heritage in Kirkwall recruits people to try to scare off barnacle geese that descend on Orkney every winter. The geese, wise to traditional scarecrows, destroy acres of pasture every year. Hogarth is one of the scarers who wave their arms and charge the geese.

• Deborah Alexander, mother of seven, medication administration technician in the cancer unit at Hackley Hospital in Muskegon, Michigan, is a locally recognized gospel singer. Although a part-time staff worker, she is also a full-time "minister of music" to the patients.

• Linda Hamilton, a Southern California mother of two,

created bar-coded cards labeled Food for All. These cards provide a convenient way for shoppers to help feed the needy. You choose how much you would like to donate, and when the clerk rings the cards up with your groceries, you end up buying food for the hungry too. Since its beginning, Food for All has raised more than $2 million for worthy groups.

• In a large Victorian home in Saranac Lake, New York, Pat Gailus has set up what is virtually a one-woman agency providing an astonishing array of social services. For instance, in one year she placed 312 battered women in safe homes, delivered 2,000 baskets of food to the hungry, gave clothing to 800 visitors, and responded to 1,800 urgent call on her telephone hot-line.

• Ian McCart is an assistant president in the New York branch of AMRO, an international bank. But every Thursday night you can find him spending an hour with each of four AIDS patients in St. Luke's-Roosevelt Hospital Center.

• Winnie, as she is known on the phone, is a volunteer at Help Line, an over-the-phone crisis intervention center in New York City. She is one of thousands of Americans who work on telephone hot-lines across the nation. They listen to the problems of the desperate, the lonely, the confused, and depressed. And because of the promise of anonymity, they are able to reach people who are afraid to talk to anyone else.

• After their son was convicted for robbery and sent to prison, Cecelia and James Whitfield of Indianapolis, Indiana, visited him regularly. The Whitfields learned that only a small percentage of the inmates received visitors, because their families found it difficult getting to the out-of-the way prisons.

The Whitfields bought a bus, recruited retired bus drivers, and set up a visitation program. On a rotating monthly schedule, the bus picks up friends and relatives of the men behind bars and visits eight different prisons.

• Karen Fox of Santa Barbara, California, dresses up like Raggedy Ann and visits patients. She gives patients some extra attention, acknowledges their special qualities, and shows affection. But most of all, she listens. People are pleased to see Raggedy Ann coming, knowing there will be no judgment.

• And certain celebrities and sports stars can move into this category. Two-time world heavy-weight champion Floyd Patterson is such a person. He is an active, "unassuming" member of several community organizations in a small upstate New York town.

The high school football field and track is named after Patterson, but not because he put a check in the mail. "That came about because the people wanted to recognize him and his work with the youth," athletic director John Ford said. "He has done a lot of work with kids in his boxing camp."

Patterson has also spent time speaking to convicts at prisons in the same area. And he is very active as an Eucharistic minister at St. Joseph's Church.

"He goes out and brings communion to the sick, people that are shut in," said Father Gregory Noel. "And he gives communion at mass. He is a very simple, unassuming, solid person. He is very quiet. He does good work for people without any show, which is a good description of his life."[7]

Every city, township, and community has special people caring for others. Many of them are volunteers. Volunteers are present everywhere—in thousands of different agencies, groups and organizations. You and your child probably meet these humanitarians and Good Samaritans every day serving in these non-profit and religious organizations. Here a listing of 100 organizations which *Money* magazine selected as the top U.S. charities, ones which have spent the highest percentage of their income on programs over the previous three years. I include this list because the charities that spend large amounts of their income on programs tend to make the best use of volunteers. And volunteers usually exemplify individuals who are caring people. They are good examples and role models for your child. Search them out and mirror their specialness to your child. In addition, your child will begin to know these charities, as most of them are mentioned in the media from time to time. As your child sees the quiet, caring individuals who serve in these charities, most likely a few of them will touch your child's life in a positive way, through heroic deeds.

Money magazine has ranked the top U.S. charities in six

major categories: social services, relief and development, education and culture, conservation, health, and religion. Here are the 100 charities listed in 1994 by category.

Relief and development

1) International Rescue Committee; 2) Mennonite Central Committee; 3) Save the Children Federation; 4) Compassion International; 5) Christian Children's Fund 6) Children International; 7) World Vision; 8) Church World Service; 9) Habitat for Humanity International; 10) U.S. Committee for UNICEF.

Social services

1) United Jewish Appeal; 2) New York Association for New Americans; 3) Neighborhood Centers; 4) American Red Cross; 5) The Arc; 6) Salvation Army; 7) Father Flanagan's Boys' Home; 8) Volunteers of America; 9) National Benevolent Association Christian Church; 10) Goodwill Industries International; 11) Catholic Charities U.S.A.; 12) Jewish Board of Family, Children's Services; 13) Children's Aid Society; 14) Boys & Girls Clubs of America; 15) Christian Appalachian Project; 16) AFS Intercultural Programs; 17) Camp Fire Boys & Girls; 18) Combined Jewish Philanthropies of Greater Boston; 19) Planned Parenthood; 20) Rotary Foundation of Rotary International; 21) Girls Inc.; 22) Boy Scouts of America; 23) Girl Scouts of America; 24) Mothers Against Drunk Driving; 25) Big Brothers/Big Sisters of America; 26) United States Olympic Committee; 27) Covenant House; 28) Disabled American Veterans; 29) Special Olympics International; 30) Hadassah, the Women's Zionist Organization; 31) YMCA of the U.S.A.; 32) YWCA of the U.S.A.

Conservation

1) National Wildlife Federation; 2) World Wildlife Fund; 3) Ducks Unlimited; 4) Nature Conservancy; 5) National Audubon Society; 6) North Shore Animal League.

Health

1) National Mental Health Association; 2) United Cerebral Palsy Associations; 3) City of Hope; 4) Muscular Dystrophy Association; 5) National Easter Seal Society; 6) Cystic Fibrosis Foundation; 7) Epilepsy Foundation of America; 8) March of Dimes; 9) American Heart Association; 10) American Lung Association; 11) American Diabetes Association; 12) American Cancer Society; 13) Arthritis Foundation; 14) National Multiple Sclerosis Society; 15) Alzheimer's Association; 16) ALSAC—St. Jude Child Research Hospital; 17) Shriners Hospital for Crippled Children.

Religion

1) The Navigators; 2) Campus Crusade for Christ; 3) Wycliffe Bible Translators; 4) Focus on the Family; 5) Billy Graham Evangelistic Association; 6) American Bible Society.

Education and culture

1) National Academy of Sciences; 2) American Council of Learned Societies; 3) Population Council; 4) Citizen's Scholarship Foundation; 5) United Negro College Fund; 6) Metropolitan Museum of Art; 7) Junior Achievement; 8) The Orchestral Association; 9) Museum Associates; 10) American Museum of Natural History; 11) Lincoln Center for Performing Arts; 12) Museum of Modern Art; 13) Philadelphia Museum of Art; 14) U.S. Holocaust Memorial Council.[8]

People doing good deeds and helpful acts are wonderful examples and role models. You hear or read about them every day. In your role of parent as hero, go one step further and share the lives and conduct of these people with your child. Be that mirror and reflect the person's helpfulness, courage, and commitment. This is good "stuff" that your child will absorb, remember, and emulate. Talk about these people; make it a daily habit. Think for a minute about someone you might have heard about today who exemplified kindness or courage—possibly someone you heard about from a neighbor, the local news, or somebody at work. Why was this person so special?

Ask your child if he or she heard of someone today that was caring, honest, or helpful. How did your child feel about this person?

Take the time to talk about these helpful people. Discuss what they did and why. Touch on the special group of people we discussed, volunteers. Why do they volunteer?

Besides the many volunteer agencies previously mentioned, another excellent example is the Olympic Games. Each year the Olympic Games involve more than 8,000 paid staff and 4,000 volunteers. Start a discussion on this group of volunteers. Here's a list to assist you in your next discussion with your child about volunteering.

Why do people volunteer? The main reason most people volunteer is because they wish to make a difference in the world, but people also volunteer for these reasons:

1. because they want to be helpful
2. because they want to improve the community
3. because they or a family member have a condition that a volunteer group supports
4. because they want to meet people
5. because they want to improve skills
6. because they need job experience
7. because they are bored
8. because their therapist has suggested they do it
9. because their probation officer has required it

10. because they are interested in the field in which they do volunteer work
11. because they need credit for a course they are taking
12. because they want to help prevent a governmental unit from spending too much money
13. because they want to learn what goes on inside a volunteer organization
14. because they are grateful for services received
15. because their boss has recommended community involvement
16. because volunteer activities enhance career resumes and college applications.[9]

Now that you are planning or have already initiated a discussion on volunteers, it is a wonderful segue to talking about your child doing volunteer work. Remember the Search Institute's criteria for positive youth development includes "being involved in prosocial behavior at least one hour per week, that is, the desire or intent to promote the welfare of others." Acts of compassion help develop social competencies, positive values and a sense of purpose in life.

Volunteering in a charitable organization gives your child a wonderful opportunity to be in the presence of "real" people helping people. Things happen when our children see, hear, and witness these humanitarians, Good Samaritans, and courageous people in action.

Here are a few examples of youth in action, most likely as a result of seeing their parents or other adults in a serving role.

• How does someone persuade teens to scrub walls in a stranger's home? According to Mark Perry, 29, who holds a Ph.D. in psychology, the key word is "Keystone." Within each of the some 1,600 Boys & Girls Clubs of America, there is a Keystone Club. Members earn points toward the annual Youth of the Year award by doing good deeds within the club framework.

• Although Sarra Jo Todd is only fourteen years old, she

spends much of her free time volunteering. As a member of Royal Roofers, she roofs houses and tackles other projects of the group. Sarra has helped rehabilitate houses for low-income families and has visited the elderly and done household chores for them. This young good Samaritan is truly a devoted volunteer. During the winter months, she sometimes works on volunteer projects all weekend. In the summer, her volunteer time extends to eight hours a day, five days a week. Why does she spend her time volunteering when she could be going to movies or watching television? Sarra volunteers because she wants to help her community. She does not like looking at vacant lots with weeds and trash; she wants her neighborhood to look nice.

In 1990, Sarra won the Youth Volunteer of the Year Award in Indianapolis, Indiana. She was selected for this honor from a total of more than four hundred volunteers in the Youth As Resources organization.[10]

And within families themselves there are children "going the extra mile."

• Jason Van Buskirk was twelve years old when his mother sent him to school to get his little sister. As he was waiting for her, several wild, vicious dogs ran across the schoolyard. At the same time a little kindergarten girl ran out the door. When one of the dogs came snarling at her, she backed off in fright.

Without any hesitation at all, Jason got in front of the little girl, gave her a push, and said, "Go back in the school." And she ran inside.

Then Jason, who was a small boy, faced the big dog. The ferocious dog leaped on Jason and bit him severely until two men, one with a wrench and another one with a pair of skates, ran up and drove the dog off.

In the hospital, a doctor said to Jason, "When you got in front of that dog and saved that sweet little girl, you were a very courageous boy."

But Jason answered, "Not really. I just didn't want the little girl to get hurt." He was more interested in her safety than his own.[11]

If someone helps a child reach his or her potential, the outcome can take the form of this child helping others and making a major impact in a community or in the world when he or she becomes an adult.

• Born to a black father and white mother in Columbus, Ohio, Barbara Harmon spent part of her childhood in Sacramento. When her parents divorced, she and her mother went on welfare.

"We just kept sliding down the economic scale. We wound up in West Virginia in a house with no running water and eventually in a house with no running water or electricity." Beside the economic problems, she had trouble being the only person of color in Doddridge County, West Virginia. At age 16, she had missed much of school because of illness and failed her junior year.

"I said I'm out of here. I don't need this. I don't have to put up with this. I'm going to get a job at the local glass factory," she told her counselor.

The counselor talked her into joining Upward Bound.

Today, Barbara Harmon-Schamberger, 31, has a law degree and is West Virginia's Secretary of Education and the Arts.[12]

"Good" people are not always blessed with happy times, but some "heroic" quiet individuals turn tough times into growth opportunities for others. Here are just a few examples of these heroes and the lasting effect they can have.

• Doug and Melissa Smith of Tulsa, Oklahoma, experienced their greatest sorrow—the death of their two-year-
old daughter. The Smith's daughter, Sunnee, died from a
rare brain tumor. In Sunnee's memory, a playground was
built for other children to enjoy. It was named Sunnee
Place.

• Friar Damien Pickel lived from June 16, 1941 to July 4,
1994. In a church bulletin, a college president shares how
special the monk was.

A tribute to Friar Damien . . .

Dear Father Damien:

I know that you may never read this letter, which I am writing as I leave for Europe. But I do need to say for you, or
for whoever finally reads these words, some of the things I
should perhaps have said to you all along. I want to thank
you for all your personal support and for the wonderful
service you have given to our students and to the College.

Personally I want to thank you for the myriad of times you
have somehow materialized in a time of crisis with a word
of comfort, usually humorous, that lightened the mood and
reassured me that the tunnel was not infinite. Thank you,
too, for your presence at my mother's funeral. You being
there meant a good deal to me.

More than any personal thanks, however, my profoundest
appreciation for all you have done for our students. I
always enjoyed seeing you holding forth in your "office" in
the cafeteria, and I know that you helped more students
than anyone can count to face up to and find solutions to
their problems and to set themselves on a forward path. For
them, too, you were a voice of good counsel and of humor
when things looked bleak. While you were not—and could

not be—an official member of our administration, I always thought of you as very much a part of our New Paltz family and I sense that you felt that way about us.

I also enjoyed seeing you interact with faculty, meeting them on their own intellectual ground with discussions of Noam Chomsky or other knotty thinkers whose meaning you like to unravel. I know how strongly you are respected and admired by many of our staff and faculty. As with the students, it is a respect and affection that you have deeply earned.

I am afraid, from what I hear today, that I shall never see you in your "office" again. But there is a little piece of New Paltz that will always be yours.
   —Alice Chandler
     President—S.U.N.Y. New Paltz, New York.[13]

In honor of the memory and example of Father Damien, the Knights of Columbus of New Paltz, New York, formed the Father Damien Pickel, OFM, Cap., Columbian Squires Circle. The purpose of the Columbian Squires is character building, while participating in social, athletic, spiritual and cultural events, as well as community service projects for teenage youth.

• Christina Vaccarino always taught her children to be kind and help people in need. They learned their lesson—perhaps too well.

Vaccarino buried one son, Edward, 11 years ago after he was knifed to death trying to stop a street robbery. She relived the tragedy when another son, Glenn Iscoe, was shot to death trying to break up a bagel shop holdup.

Vaccarino said she will use her experiences to lobby for tighter gun control laws.

- When Linda Bremmer's 10-year-old son Andy died of cancer, she came across Andy's address book with the names of 20 children he had met at a summer camp for cancer patients. The book reminded Linda of how much Andy had enjoyed receiving mail, and how he had been deluged with cards and letters while in the hospital but received none when he came home.

Because of this, she started "Love Letters," a unique ministry of letter-writing to terminally and chronically ill children. There are over 620 children on Linda's list. Linda writes each letter herself, and with the help of a volunteer staff and other people who donate cards and trinkets, each youngster receives a newsletter and another piece of mail each month.

- "It's all right," 15-year-old Tiffany assured her parents as they rushed her 11-year-old brother, Michael, to the San Angelo (Texas) hospital in the family car.

Less than 24 hours later, Michael died. Through Michael's death, Tiffany had discovered how precious—and fragile—life is, and how vital it is to the healing process to look for ways to help others.

She became a leader in her senior class, and helped organize a chapter of Students in Texas Against Narcotics and Drinking. She was a counselor at The Hole in the Wall Gang Camp, a summer camp for terminally ill kids in Connecticut. Tiffany also did volunteer work at a Lubbock Hospital's critical-care ward for children.

A few years later, Tiffany Talley completed an internship at the Children's Medical Center in Dallas. In her new career as a social worker, she will be constantly reminded of her brother's death. Yet, it's not death that drives her on, but the joy of life. And she spreads that joy to everyone she touches.[14]

The following story is one of dual heroes—an adult providing help for a child and the child in return becoming an inspiration to his school and community.

• Applause thundered through the Snoqualmie Valley (Washington) school auditorium as Ryan Shewell walked across the stage. "I'm proud to present you with this President's Fitness Award," his physical education teacher said. "You chewed through those times of frustration and doubt, and met everything squarely."

Just a few months earlier, Ryan had lost both legs below the knee and the fingers on both hands to a rare blood disease. Now he reached out to accept a symbol of his perseverance and faith.[15]

During this ordeal there were many supportive people including his parents and the many doctors and nurses, but there was also another especially kind person.

Two weeks after having both legs amputated, the baseball coach from Ryan's school brought him a cap, ball, and jersey from the team—and encouragement. The coach had had both feet amputated. He removed his artificial feet and put them on Ryan's bed. "They're great for saving places in the bleachers at a game," the coach said. Then he replaced the prostheses. "Ryan," he said, "you'll be able to do all the things you did before."

After the coach left, Ryan sat quietly in the bed. Finally he said, "You know, Mom, before Coach came, I thought my legs would grow back. But it's okay. These are my legs now, and they'll work. And Coach said I can still play soccer."[16]

Who are these adult and child heroes and where do they reside? Cliff Schimmels describes his discovery while working for a weekly newspaper in a small, country town in West Texas.

One day I told my publisher, "There is nothing left to write."

"Let me tell you an important truth," his publisher replied. "Every one of those people out there is an important person with an interesting story. If you are any kind of newspaper person, you will go out and discover some of those stories."

In my search, I learned an important lesson. Almost every person I meet qualifies as a big person, and each one deserves our interest, our attention and our respect.

The most interesting thing about all these everyday heroes is that they don't think they are big people.

The lesson for all of us is obvious. The first requirement of being a hero is not to think that you are one.[17]

The world is full of helping and caring individuals.

Since 1990, *USA Weekend* magazine, The Points of Light Foundation, and its local Volunteer Centers have coordinated a national day of service, Make a Difference Day. This past year, over 500,000 people across the country and abroad were inspired to pitch in on projects large and small.

Awards include 10 outstanding projects receiving $2,000 for a charity they select along with participation in National Volunteer Week activities in Washington, D.C. There are also 50 honorable-mention projects which each receive $2,000 for their favorite charity.

A few of the 1994 projects included: Six adults with severe retardation helping homeless in Louisville; 1,000 members and friends of the Student Conservation Association beautifying state parks, school grounds, and community centers in New Hampshire; U.S. Navy volunteers stationed at Southern Europe NATO headquarters in Naples, Italy, launching a food drive for orphanages; A group of women raising money to buy a dictionary for each child in Beaufort, North Carolina; and thousands of Girl Scouts and leaders holding hospital baby showers in Houston.[18]

Youth who care about others are in each and every community. The Christophers is just one of the many organizations that sponsor literary contests for high school students to express the good in people. The Christophers in New York City holds an annual poster contest. Students in grades 9 through 12 are invited to interpret the theme of "You Can Make A Difference" and create an original poster. *Guideposts* Magazine is another organization that sponsors a writing contest for teenagers. *Guideposts* Young Writers contest asks high school juniors and seniors to write an honest account of a true-life personal experience. The contest guidelines tell the students that their story need not be highly dramatic or unusual, but that it should be about an experience that touched them deeply, one that changed them. They are to write about something that happened at home, at school, at a job or on a trip. And they are told not to be shy about describing their feelings.

Guideposts receives between 5000 and 9000 manuscripts annually from youths who perform good deeds, overcome tough situations, and assist others in need.

Each and every community recognizes these helping individuals in some way. I'm on the Good Samaritan committee for Putnam County, New York. A Good Samaritan Award is for an individual who has enhanced the quality of life in the local community, someone with a concern for others, who has given of himself or herself without compensation. There are many, many people who are the quiet, unsung heroes. Contact your local community agency to find out about recognition programs in your area.

I remember interviewing a woman named Emma and asking her what her goals were. She looked perplexed and responded with "I don't think I have any goals." I was shocked and set aback with this response. I thought to myself, "What kind of person doesn't have goals?"

Well, a few years later, Emma passed away in her sleep, a very unexpected but peaceful death. Over one hundred people turned out for a memorial service where she worked and many more came to her funeral. Again I was shocked but I understood. Emma was a quiet hero to many. She was kind and kindhearted. Her "goal" was the everyday task of helping others, both young and old, in a very serene way. Emma loved children and would demonstrate this love in a variety of ways, including dressing up as animal characters for holiday parties.

For adults, Emma would write personal letters with uplifting messages. Even years after her death, the staff at her last employer still receives a letter or card from people across the United States thanking her for her care and concern.

These special people are all around us. You could use the term unsung heroes, some people might even describe them as angels, but most are big people, good Samaritans, and humanitarians. Talk about them, meet them, have your child be around people like this—in human service organizations, for example.

They are different than celebrities because they are reachable—they don't charge for signing an autograph or usually don't take hours to prepare themselves in dress and make-up. They are different from historical figures because they are usually alive and present today and they help others on a one-to-one basis.

These people are wonderful role models for character development, values, and good deeds. They help us realize we can make a difference. Be that mirror reflecting the good deeds of these people. Doing so will inspire and help prepare your child for adulthood, and it will continue to strengthen the bond between the two of you.

People seldom improve when they have no other model but themselves to copy.
    —Oliver Goldsmith (1730–1774)
    British Poet, Dramatist, Author

9

Heroes or Teachers?

Mentors and Life Coaches

Example is not the main thing in influencing others—it is the only thing.
—Albert Schweitzer (1875 -1965)
French Missionary, Physician

Jim is a volunteer. Jim is not only giving back to the school community by being on the Board of Education, but he's a mentor. Now that his two daughters are in college, Jim has made the decision to be a Big Brother to Jason. I see them playing ball, working in the garden, changing the oil in the car, and many times just sitting and talking.

Jim has become a mentor, also known as a teacher, a friend, an adult companion. Jim is definitely making a difference in Jason's life. A hero? By using my definition of "a hero performs a deed that provides a meaningful, positive change in someone," Jim is a hero. Mentors provide young people with support, learning opportunities, and positive youth development. Mentors, teachers, and life "coaches" can be heroes.

According to a Search Institute study, there are five categories of mentoring programs. These programs are

1. traditional such as Big Brother/Big Sister
2. long-term focused activity such as tutoring or career mentors
3. short-term focused activity such as in-school tutoring or summer internships
4. team mentoring such as kinship programs

5. group mentoring, which includes Girl Scout leaders
    who are being seen as mentors

The conclusion of the study states that mentoring is a win-win situation. Just within the five programs which participated in the "Understanding Mentoring Relationships" study, over one thousand volunteers were working with over 1800 young people in significant, beneficial, and most certainly cost-effective relationships. Young people win; adult volunteers win. It is, quite frankly, society at large that is eventually the real winner.[1]

A million dollar experiment on mentoring, financed by the Ford Foundation in four American cities, has now produced some of the most remarkable results for poor youth since the test runs for Head Start and Job Corps. The experiment, known as the Quantum Opportunities Program, stands out for its common sense: What poor children from crumbled families and neighborhoods need most is an adult who cares about them and sticks with them for years.

One of these mentors, Reuben Mills, embarked on a four-year odyssey with 25 ninth graders. He would serve as their father, big brother or friend, or whatever was needed to keep them in high school, out of trouble, and on the road to college.

Nineteen of Mr. Mill's 25 students graduated from high school and 18 went on to college or training schools, compared with only 12 graduates and 7 college-bound students in a control group of youths from the same school who did not participate.[2]

Planned mentoring programs for adolescents are, by definition, structured, and their goals can be complex, ambitious, and even grandiose—preventing students from becoming pregnant, dropping out of school, or going to jail; helping them make a successful transition from high school to college; or giving them some undefined but dramatically better chance at life.

There are certain essential elements in mentoring relationships for youth:

The first is creating a supportive relationship between a

youth or young adult and someone more senior in age and experience who offers support, guidance, and concrete assistance as the younger partner goes through a difficult period, enters a new area of experience, takes on an important task, or corrects an earlier problem. During mentoring, mentees identify with their mentors; as a result, they become more able to do for themselves what their mentors have done for them.

In their instrumental roles, mentors act as teachers, advisers, coaches, advocates, and dispensers and sharers of concrete resources.[3]

It is not only the poor, minority, institutionalized, or even the young that benefit from mentors. Mentors, teachers, and coaches can be helpful throughout one's lifetime. Although typical mentoring programs are for teenagers, there are many mentoring programs for adults, even within major organizations. The Planned Giving Group of Greater New York on its membership application asks these two questions:

1. Would a mentor in gift planning be helpful to you?
2. Would you be a mentor in gift planning for another development professional?

As your child grows older, there will be other adults besides you in his or her life who will make a major impact. These significant others may include mentors, which might include teachers and even other students. *World Almanac's* Heroes of Young Americans poll included the question of naming "the person most directly influential in your life, other than your parents." The students split their votes evenly between teachers and friends.

Let's take a look at some examples of both of these groups as well as parents in this role.

Teachers making a difference

The Walt Disney company annually promotes and presents the American Teachers Awards. In a full-page ad, it states "We'd like to introduce you to some role models who don't dunk basketballs over giants for a living . . . After all, you don't have to be 7 feet tall to have a child look up to you." These awards presented on national television, recognize the importance of teachers in the lives of youths.

EduQuest, the IBM Educational Systems Company, and USA Today's Educational Initiatives Department celebrate the National PTA's Teacher Appreciation Week. They thank the more than 2. 8 million educators who have made the challenge of educating our nation's youth their most important priority. Testimonies from celebrities on how a teacher has made a difference in their lives include:

> I suppose one of the most memorable episodes that occurred between a teacher and myself was the saving of a drawing that I did, made in Miss Paro's class when I was in high school. Our assignment was to draw any objects that came in mind in groups of three. The object, of course, was to produce creativity. Twenty-five years later, I received this drawing from Miss Paro with a note telling me that she had been saving it. This was one of the few positive examples of faith in me that I experienced.[4]
>
> —Charles M. Schultz, creator of the comic strip, Peanuts

LeConte Junior High was huge. Too huge. A million kids. I used to spend my whole lunch hour wishing I was back with Mrs. Ernst, my sixth grade teacher, at Selma Avenue Grammar School. She was my favorite teacher. If our sixth grade had been extra good that week, she'd spend the last hour or so on Fridays reading to us. She was a wonderful actress and she threw herself into the stories and became all the characters—accents and everything. I remember she read "The Yearling" to us. It was the story of a young boy, Jody, who lived in the backwoods of some southern state with his parents a long time ago. It was a story about his love for his pet, a wild fawn named Flag. It was a story about growing up and learning to shoulder responsibility, Mrs. Ernst said. When she got to the part where Flag had to be shot, she "became" Jody, and she started crying real tears and screamed the way a real little kid would. She turned into him right before our eyes. I thought it was a swell thing to be able to do. I think she was responsible for my choosing an acting career.[5]

  —Carol Burnett, motion picture, stage & television
   actress

When I was a youngster growing up in the ghetto of Buffalo, New York, there was a man named Lorrie Alexander who really turned my life around. He, along with my parents, started me on the way to positive self-esteem, feeling good about who I was, and also understanding that nothing in life comes easy—you have to outwork the other guy to have a chance for success. Mr. Alexander, as head of the Boys Club, affected not only my life but thousands of other young men and women who could have gone the other way. Yes, he touched my life and now, I use those same words to make a difference with young people in our NBA Stay in School Program. I'm living proof you can make a difference—just try.[6]

  —Bob Lanier, Chairperson, NBA Stay in School
   Program and 1992 inductee, Basketball Hall of Fame

As with the quiet and unsung heroes in the previous chapter, teachers are also recognized on a local level by their community. In the area where I live, we have a recognition program for the "Teacher of the Month" honoring excellence in the classroom. Besides teaching skills, this excellence involves relating to the students, enhancing and broadening their experiences, and providing emotional support.

Peers as mentors

While for many students, teachers have a major impact on their lives, for others it may be a fellow classmate or peer. Research by the U.S. Department of Education shows that "tutoring other students can lead to improved academic achievement for both student and tutor, and to positive attitudes toward coursework." Tutoring programs consistently raise the achievement of both the students receiving instruction and those providing it. Peer tutoring, when used as a supplement to regular classroom teaching, helps slow and underachieving students master their lessons and succeed in school. Preparing and giving the lessons also benefits the tutors themselves because they learn more about the material they are teaching.[7]

In San Antonio, 45 percent of Hispanic students drop out of school before graduating from high school; more than half of these youth leave before ninth grade. To stop this loss, the Intercultural Development and Research Association (IDRA), a local organization, designed the Values Youth Partnership Program to engage potential dropouts, train them as tutors, and assign each tutor to three to five students at adjacent elementary schools.

The rationale for the program is twofold. First, IDRA research determined that teachers could spot students at risk of dropping out through a combination of declining grades, rising absenteeism, and increasing behavior problems. Second, a review of numerous studies of cross-age tutoring showed that tutors made significant gains in achievement, even greater than did tutees.[8]

An 18-year-old freshman at East Texas State University has been named National Youth of the Year by the Boys & Girls Clubs of America. LaWanda Jones is the first black woman to win the honor that includes a $10,000 scholarship from the Reader's Digest Association Inc.

Jones' home life has been severely affected by drug abuse since she was 12. She joined the West Dallas Boys & Girls Club almost three years ago and credits it with building her self-esteem and leadership skills.

"That club and its staff are like adoptive parents that have raised this street kid to be the confident and very motivated person I am today," says Jones.

"I enjoy being a living testament to the younger children, demonstrating that not only can you survive hard times, but you can succeed through them," she says.[9]

Whether it be the winner of the high school Science Fair, a writing contest, or a bake-off, there are excellent peer examples and role models within each school. As you focus on preparing a young teen for college, think about having him or her associate with or be mentored by an honor roll student. Or have the child associate with a college student, thereby helping the child better understand and prepare for furthering his or her education. If you think peer mentoring might be helpful, talk with teachers and guidance counselors and keep a continuous watch for other mentoring student possibilities.

Parent support

Mentoring focuses on learning. If you continue focusing on education and improving your child's scholastic level, you can naturally fit into this role of advisor, advocate, or mentor. If you are open to this opportunity, it is an exciting new facet of parenting to pursue as your child matures.

Researchers at the International Center for the Advancement of Scientific Literacy in Chicago determined that parents don't need to be highly educated themselves to interest their children in science and math. "The single largest influence is if parents indicate that they would like their children to go to higher levels of education and let them know they (parents) care about it."[10]

The ultimate goal is to assist your child in obtaining a well-rounded education. The key is to show interest and support without being overwhelming. A good way to begin this process is to find out what your child's special interest or expertise is and build on this. Before we contemplate this issue, take a few minutes and think of the people who inspired you in pursuing your various interests and vocation.

Teachers? _____

Peers? _____

Family Members? _____

Other Individuals? _____

Now what have you seen your child express interest in? Has your child completed any interest surveys or questionnaires—what areas came out on top?

_____

_____

Is there someone he or she is admiring or looking up to regarding this attraction?

_____

_____

Find out what your child's interests are and then find someone who can mentor him or her. A step before finding a mentor might be to unveil a role model in your child's life. It may be helpful here to clarify the distinction between role models and mentors. Role models can be people your child knows or other individuals they have come in contact with or read about in a magazine or newspaper. A mentor is someone who takes an active role in a younger person's life, serving as a guide, counselor, teacher, and friend who believes in you and tries to help you succeed. Sometimes a child does not want or need a mentor but may have a role model, other than a parent, that he or she looks up to.

Think about role models on a grander scale, particularly people who have won achievement awards in specific areas. Below is a listing of special awards in addition to ones mentioned in previous chapters. Become familiar with some of these. One of them might be what interests your child. Bring it to his or her attention. Make your child aware of these award winners. Encourage your child to read about them, maybe even write to them. Let these people be an inspirational-type of mentor.

Being around these individuals obviously is the best form of mentoring but just learning about these people can be a positive influence. All options and opportunities should be considered when it comes to supporting your child's continuing education. Although just reading about these individuals is somewhat distant and broad-based, it can still be inspiring nonetheless.

Educational role models and mentors might include New York's Best & Brightest Community College Students, students who have a minimum cumulative grade point average of 3.25 on a scale of 4.0. Judges consider grades, academic awards, leadership roles on and off campus, and community service. And on a national level, *USA Today* salutes the college all-stars, the 20 college students on the All-USA Academic First Team, representatives of the wide diversity of talent on the nation's campuses.

Other award winners may be of interest to your child. Discuss these award recipients as a steppingstone to finding your child's area of interest, role model, or possible mentor. If you begin to get excited and interested, this will "rub off" on your child. Remember, show your child you care about your child's interests, endeavors, and his or her future.

Special awards for books:
- Academy of American Poets Awards given by the Fellowship for Distinguished Poetic Achievement.
- Hans Christian Anderson Awards, every 2 years for important contribution to children's literature.
- Bollingen Prize in Poetry by Yale Library for lifetime achievement.
- Booker Prize, British award for fiction.
- Caldecott Medal by American Library Association for most distinguished American picture book.
- Christopher Awards by The Christophers for expression of highest values of human spirit.
- Curtis Benjamin Award for Creative Publishing by Association of American Publishers.
- Golden Kite Awards by Society of Children's Book Writers and Illustrators.
- International Fiction Prize by Irish Times and Aer Lingus for work of fiction published in Ireland, U.K., or U.S.

- Kingsley Tufts Poetry Prize by Claremont Graduate School.
- Ruth Lilly Poetry Prize by Modern Poetry Association and American Council for the Arts, lifetime achievement.
- Lincoln Prize by Lincoln Soldiers Institute at Gettysburg College for lifetime contribution to Civil War studies.
- National Book Awards by National Book Foundation.
- National Book Critics Circle Awards.
- Newbery Award by American Library Association for most distinguished contribution to American literature for children.
- Francis Parkman Prize by Society of American Historians for scholarship combined with literary excellence.
- PEN/Faulkner Award for Fiction.
- Edgar Allan Poe Awards by Mystery Writers of America.
- Rhea Award for the Short Story by Dungannon Foundation for lifetime achievement.
- Society of American Historians—Francis Parkman Prize, Bruce Catton Prize for Lifetime Achievement, and Allan Nevins Dissertation Prize.
- Whiting Writers' Awards by Whiting Foundation for achievement and promise alike.

Special awards for journalism:

- Helen B. Bernstein Award by New York Public Library.
- National Journalism Awards by Scripps Howard Foundation for print journalism.
- National Magazine Awards by American Society of Magazine Editors and Columbia University School of Journalism.
- George Polk Awards by Long Island University for excellence in journalism.
- Reubon Awards by National Cartoonists Society.
- Science in Society Print Journalism Awards by National Association of Science Writers.

- John Peter Zenge Award by the University of Arizona for distinguished service in behalf of freedom of press.

Special awards for entertainment—
movie, TV, radio, and theater:

- Astaire Awards for achievement in dance in Broadway theater by Theater Development Fund.
- Susan Smith Blackburn Awards for female playwright.
- Christopher Awards for movies and TV specials by The Christophers.
- Directors Guild of America for a variety of TV acknowledgement.
- Drama Desk Awards by New York theater critics writing for non-New York publications.
- Alfred I. Dupont-Columbia University Awards for broadcast journalism.
- Emmy Awards, Daytime and Prime-Time by Academy of Television Arts and Sciences.
- National Society of Film Critics for a variety of film awards.
- New York Drama Critics Circle awards.
- Tony (Antoinette Perry) Awards.

Miscellaneous special awards:

- American Institute of Architects Gold Medal.
- James Beard Awards for chef of the year, restaurant of the year, outstanding service, lifetime achievement, and rising star.
- Breakthrough Awards by Women and Media for influencing change in gender stereotypes.
- Charles Frankel Prizes by National Endowment for the Humanities for those who have increased public awareness of humanities.
- Gavel Award by American Bar Association for lifetime achievement.
- John F. Kennedy Center for the Performing Arts Awards for contribution to U.S. cultural life.

- Library of the Year Award by Gale Research, Inc. and *Library Journal.*
- McGraw-Hill Prize in Education for distinguished contribution to the advancement of education.
- National Inventors Hall of Fame induction.
- National Medal of Arts by White House for outstanding contribution to cultural life in the U.S.
- Pritzker Architecture Prize by the Hyatt Foundation.
- Rock-and-Roll Hall of Fame induction.
- Samuel H. Scipps American Dance Festival Award.
- Teacher of the Year by the Council of Chief State School Officers and Encyclopedia Britannica.
- Templeton Prize for Progress in Religion.
- Van Cliburn International Piano Competition.
- Westinghouse Talent Search.[11]

Now bring this interest and role model back to your child's life and education. Assist your children in understanding that they, too, can excel in a certain field and be recognized for their efforts. If further education is the goal and your child has a special interest, pursuing a scholarship may be a great incentive, both financially and mentally. I recommend reviewing *The Scholarship Directory, Minority Guide to Scholarships and Financial Aid* (available through Tinsley Communications, 804-723-4499) offering hundreds of listings for possible scholarships. Minority may mean having a particular cultural background or a specialized field of study—architecture majors, high school seniors planning a career in teaching, family member of an active duty member of the United States Armed Forces, nursing students, and qualified American Indian high school juniors.

Mentoring and learning involve being motivated and inspired by others whether by being aware of someone winning a special award in a subject your child is interested in or through a direct intervention by an adult to help a child mature and develop.

Non-sport coaching

During the 90's a new type of mentor has evolved—the coach. It is a new profession pertaining to counseling and consulting someone in the various aspects of life, work, and relationships. Coaches assist their clients, usually college-age and adults, in their learning and growing.

Thomas J. Leonard, Founder, Coach University, Utah, has been one of the leaders in this field. He explains the role of coach in this manner:

"A Coach is your partner in achieving professional goals, your champion during a turnaround, your trainer in communication and life skills, your sounding board when making choices, your motivator when strong actions are called for, your unconditional support when you take a hit, your mentor in personal development, your co-designer when developing an extraordinary project, your beacon during stormy times, your wake-up call if you don't hear your own, and most importantly:

Your coach is your partner in living the life you know you're ready for, personally and professionally."[12]

Denis Waitley, renowned motivational speaker and author, offers professional coaching on an intensive three-month basis. And the national training company CareerTrack offers a course entitled "Practical Coaching Skills for Managers."

Annette Covatta of Carmel, New York, enables persons to reach their potential and become their authentic selves. She helps people tap their inner strength in facing life's crossroads; release the trivial and embrace what really matters; get past fears and anxieties; explore dreams; leave behind negativity; integrate loss and grief and move on; and get access to their unique process of growth and learn to trust it.

Parents as coaches

Mentoring and coaching are similar in the processes they employ. Research on "Mentoring in Action" by

Columbia University in New York shows good mentors have motivation, personal commitment, realistic or high expectations, flexibility, respect for the individual's right to make choices, firmness, supportive tendencies, and good listening skills.

William J. Bennett offers some helpful advice for parents in this area in his book, *The Book of Virtues*: "How do we encourage our children to persevere, to persist in their efforts to improve themselves, their own lot, and the lot of others? By standing by them, and with them and behind them; by being coaches and cheerleaders, and by the witness of our own example."[13]

Linda Ching Sledge tells about her experience regarding "being there" instead of taking an active part in her child's endeavors.

In the first two lonely months of college, Tim called home often for advice. I urged him to find a congenial group to make his adjustment to campus life easier. Finally, in early November, he phoned with good news.

"I'm rushing a fraternity. We're down to the last fifty guys, and the 'brothers' say I have a great chance of getting in. I'll know for sure Sunday night after the voting."

"Terrific," I replied, feeling my own spirits soar at his excitement. "Call me when the votes are in."

Yet Sunday night came, and Tim did not call. Monday and Tuesday passed the same way. It wasn't until Wednesday that the phone rang.

"I didn't get in," he said, sounding tired and strained.

Although the news was no surprise, I still felt his disappointment as keenly as if someone had slammed a fist into my stomach. My mother instinct warned me to tread carefully, but unwisely I blurted out, "You didn't call!"

"No," he replied carefully. "I needed to work things out by myself."

He didn't need me? Me? His mother? Who had picked him up when he fell? Who had wiped away his childhood tears and listened to his boyhood laments? Reproachful words rose to my lips, but before I could utter them, he said, "I just signed up to audition for a men's barbershop chorus. Two hundred guys are trying, too. . . ."More wistfully he added, "You think I've got a chance?"

I heard the need in his voice. This time I heeded my mother instinct, which told me exactly what to say, "Go for it! And call me when the votes are in."[14]

Another terrific story is by Sean Coxe of West Chester, Pennsylvania. I am not sure where I came across this story, but it is a wonderful example of the role of parent as coach.

As a child, I could always depend on my father to put life's disasters into perspective, whether it was a broken leg or a broken heart. Years later I was devastated by a series of personal crises. Feeling helpless and overwhelmed, I spent my last $300 on a trip to Florida to see Dad.

On the final evening of my visit we stood at the end of a jetty, watching the sun settle into the Gulf of Mexico. I could no longer contain my bitterness.

"You know, Dad, if we could take all the great moments we experience in our lifetimes and put them back-to-back, they wouldn't last twenty minutes."

He responded simply, "Yup."
I turned to him, stunned. He was still studying the sun that sat on the horizon. Then, looking, evenly into my eyes, he added quietly, "Precious, aren't they?"

Once a week, on Tuesday mornings, Becky Moser drives to school, puts on her volunteer badge and spends an hour with a student. Moser is a mentor in her local school system.

Moser reveals, "I don't know if I am going to make a big difference in her life, really. But I've given her something. I have told her she is worth my trouble. I have told her that I like to listen to her stories, that I like being with her, that she's important to me.[15]

Sound familiar? Like being a parent? I think we have come full circle. Mentors and coaches help children mature, grow, and learn. They are teachers. They perform deeds that provide meaningful, positive changes in young adults. And that is also what a parent does in an ongoing way. Parents are mentors, teachers, coaches, and more—they are #1 heroes.

Johnny Bench, former Cincinnati Reds catcher, and member of the Baseball Hall of Fame, summarizes the significance of teachers and parents as mentors and coaches:

> Binger, Oklahoma is a small suburb of 661 people and, to a schoolboy, was blessed with so many fine teachers and educators. To pick one seems a bit unfair, because each one gave me special incentive to learn and excel in life. A man who stands out is Hugh Haley. Mr. Haley, known as "Soch" (short for sociable), was the Jr. High principal and math teacher. There are classroom lessons and life lessons, and my days spent learning algebra and nights traveling to sporting events throughout Oklahoma will be treasured forever.

> My best teachers, and hopefully each young person's, were my parents Ted and Katy. I hope all parents will accept that responsibility.[16]

As your child matures, your control, assistance, and direction of your child's actions lessens significantly but a new opportunity opens up, one of coach. You've given your child life, whether biologically or through adoption. You've protected your child as an infant and toddler and raised him or her through childhood and adolescence. You continue to give unconditional love for a lifetime as a parent and also as a friend. You remain a hero, the highest level of a hero. But one of the most valuable things you can do now when your child is growing up, is to just be there. Be a mirror, but this time to reflect the skills and talents of your child. After all these years of doing things for your child, you need to be still and know that you have been and always will be a big part of your child's life. Now your role continues as supporter and coach.

When you give away some of the light from the candle, there isn't less light because you've given some away—there's more. When everyone grows, there isn't less of anybody, there's more of—and for—everybody.
　　　　　—Kaleel Jamison
　　　　　Author

10

Heroism—Deeds, Decency, and Endurance

Heroism consists in hanging on one minute longer.
—Norwegian Proverb

Ryan and Zachary were excited. They awoke early on that Sunday morning. We needed to leave our house at 7:30 am because the buses were leaving at 8 am for New York City. Our family was going on a day trip to visit the National Museum of the American Indian and also the Museum of Natural History. The day proved to be very busy and entertaining but little did I know that this trip would resemble a microcosm of what this book is all about. Let me explain.

The Indian Museum was informative and contained both historical and mythological offerings. Displays and artifacts showed how the Indians used to live, and a room was set up showing how the contemporary Indian lives. Totem poles and drawings of animals portrayed the Indian's deeply felt communion with nature.

After leaving the Indian Museum, the group stopped for lunch. We ended up at Planet Hollywood, a restaurant with hand prints of movies stars on the outside walls and movie paraphernalia inside. Waiting to be seated, we looked around and were impressed by the various costumes and stage props of celebrities such as Arnold Schwarzenager and Bruce Willis. We ordered the $12 hamburgers but declined on purchasing the $38 Planet Hollywood sunglasses and the $325 leather jacket.

The two buses continued on to the Museum of Natural History. Although we toured the museum on our own, there were volunteer guides at the different levels. The one volunteer guide stamped Ryan and Zachary's museum book and made sure the boys promised to go look at the Chinese wedding chair. We searched the area and were delighted when we located this item of beauty. How thoughtful of this person to spend time here at the museum getting children excited and interested in the different exhibits.

Driving home on the bus we talked with the coordinators of the trip—a husband and wife who run a tutoring school. Ryan attends the school during the summer to keep his academic skills at high levels. As we talked with the teachers, we realized it would be helpful to have Ryan tested for his reading, writing, and math skills and we set up an appointment to have the testing done.

During this one day's outing we came in contact with all the types of individuals discussed in chapters 6 through 9—celebrities, historical characters, volunteers, and teachers. This trip to New York City confirmed that the hero concept is prevalent in a positive way throughout our society each and every day.

The heroes discussed in the previous four chapters—celebrities and sports stars, historical and mythological characters, Good Samaritans and courageous people, and mentors and coaches—are surfacing everywhere, and that's good, because we need them.

In the book, *The Great Deeds of Superheroes*, Maurice Saxby and Robert Ingpen tell why heroes are important in today's society. They point out that in our imperfect society, with its increasing demands to achieve success in study, sports or work, we need to be reassured by stories of a world where all things are possible if we are brave enough, strong and wise enough. We need inner strength to deal with the problems of being human and we need shining examples in our search for the meaning and value of life and for our moral development.[1]

Heroes are evident in our lives on a daily basis. A few examples include:

- A two-year-old boy is recovered, blue and lifeless, from a pond, thanks to the combined effort of someone pulling him out, an off-duty firefighter starting the boy breathing, and two off-duty nurses helping him revive the boy.
- NBC makes a 15-second television announcement thanking teachers for all they do.
- An individual is named National Superintendent of the Year by the American Association of School Administrators.
- A New York paper lists New York's 100 Freshest Faces, all up-and-comers under 40 who are making their mark in the world's toughest, most competitive city.
- A major insurance company presents their Good Neighbor Award to a seventh-grade teacher
- An article tells "Why Superheroes can be good for kids."
- A teenager receives a press pass to cover the Oscars as a reporter and "hobnob with the rich and famous."
- A politician tries to make his mark in history by making a dynamic speech and proposing a new economic recovery program.
- Over 7,200 athletes from 141 nations compete in the Special Olympics World Games.
- A magazine article depicts "TV's Most Powerful Stars" and "Hollywood's Big Spenders."
- Topps Company sells a baseball card series called, "All-Time Heroes of Baseball."
- A book helps movie lovers locate film locations and celebrity hangouts.
- Another sports star comes out of retirement for a multi-million contract.
- A 19-year-old man is elected mayor of a small upstate town.
- A major sports equipment company recognizes individuals for their community work with youngsters.
- A new national anti-violence program for communities is created.

- A blind man attempts to scale Denali, the 20,320-foot north peak of Alaska's Mount McKinley.
- The College Academic All-Stars for this year are named.
- *Reader's Digest* honors 10 educators with the "American Heroes in Education" Awards.

Some of this information is national news, some local, but it can all be very exciting and intriguing to your child if he or she is made aware of these happenings. As you begin to look for more and more positive role models and kind people, you will see they are everywhere. Besides television and newspapers, there are many other resources for information about these news-breaking individuals. Some of these resources are encyclopedias (even on CD-ROM), books, magazines, videos, teachers, cassettes, statues, museums, computer on-line chats and forums, newsletters, schools, churches, seminar and workshops, and trading cards.

As a parent, mirror these people for their special characteristic or feat. But before you mirror people from the media or other reference materials, remind yourself of the first insight.

Understand Who Your Child's #1 Hero and Role Model is—YOU!

You are not competing with these media heroes so relax, and be confident in relating to your child. This will help you feel less threatened by some of these people and you can concentrate more on your child's development and relationship with you.

To help lay to rest any remaining doubts about your child's deep-rooted fascination with sports stars and celebrities, here are three more supporting indicators that show how celebrities are not major influencers for our children, that individuals from your community are your child's role models and mentors, and that parents are the real heroes.

Celebrities are not heroes, maybe not even role models

David Elkind, Ph.D., a professor of child study at Tufts University and author of various parenting books, studied young people regarding rock stars and found a surprising discovery: Antisocial rock- and rap-music stars are clearly not their role models. When he talked to the students about other, more socially responsible musicians, the students did not see them as role models either. Although younger teenagers often develop strong emotional ties to pop idols, this is more a sign of their newly discovered status as teenagers than it is of any serious identification with say, Guns N' Roses or Snoop Doggy Dog.

Elkind says that youths who do identify with such anarchistic performers, and who adopt their values and attitudes, are youth who are already troubled and adrift. These teenagers are often the victims of neglect, abandonment, and abuse.

Elkind followed up his personal findings with a Gallup poll of young people that reinforced his viewpoint. When asked to name the person they most admired, the majority chose a parent or some other relative. [2]

Adults are role models

Here is a not-so-surprising U.S. Department of Education research finding: Good character is encouraged by surrounding students with good adult examples and by building upon natural occasions for learning and practicing good character. Skillful educators know how to organize their schools, classrooms, and lessons to foster such examples.

The home, the school, and the community all contribute to a child's character development. Children learn character traits such as honesty, courtesy, diligence, and respect for others, in part, from examples set by their parents, teachers, peers, and the community as a whole.

Schools can reinforce good character by how they organize and present themselves, how the adults conduct themselves, and how standards for behavior and integrity are set and enforced.

Educators become good role models through their professionalism, courtesy, cooperation, and by demanding top performance from their students.

And teachers can use examples from life and literature to nurture qualities of good character and ethical behavior.[3]

Parents are heroes

John McDermott, M.D., professor of child psychiatry at the University of Hawaii School of Medicine, sums up his research on heroes with this statement: "In all my years of practice, I have never known a child to be permanently scarred by losing a media hero. Remember, you are your child's most important hero, even if it doesn't always feel like that."[4]

A review of your role of parent as hero

First, know you can make a difference, even as one person. Diane MacEacherns makes this point in her book, *Save Our Planet, 750 Everyday Ways You Can Help Clean Up The Earth*. She talks about each person helping our environment, but I think her message can be applied to parenting as well.

> "Even though you are just one person who may never have done anything extraordinary before, you can change the world.

> It's not that corporations, the government, or legislators should be let off the hook: We must demand a cleaner, safer environment and a healthier world, and we must hold industry and government accountable for the many actions they take that affect the health of the earth and the future of the planet.

> But we're responsible, too. This is our world, and it's the only one we've got. By making small but substantial deci-

sions about the things we do, the goods we buy, and the laws we support, we can make a better life for ourselves while helping to ensure a world that's fit for the future. If we expect others to be accountable, then we must be held accountable, too, starting with our own lives."[5]

You can make a difference in the development of your child, your family, and society.

The second part of your role as hero is performing deeds. Celebrities are idols not heroes. Historical and mythological figures are famous personalities. Good Samaritans can be heroes, but most likely are kind people. Mentors teach your child and help them grow. Mentors most likely are heroes but parents definitely are the #1 heroes.

Now that you understand your status of hero, this does not mean you need to gloat about your role nor strive to be a supermom or superdad. The main thing parents as heroes need to do is perform deeds that will assist your child in developing. These deeds are reflected in the other four insights discussed in chapters 2 through 5.

2. Know and share your values—demonstrate them.
3. Strengthen your child's self-esteem and family-esteem.
4. Talk with your child—and more important, listen.
5. Examine your child's environment, determine what you can do to enhance or if necessary, change it, and teach your child about choices and consequences that relate to your child's well-being.

Obviously each one of these insights demands a great deal of dedication and commitment, but our children need and want it. Youth are telling adults and researchers that they want to be close to their parents. A 1995 survey by KidsPeace—a non-profit group that offers parenting advice—of 1,023 children ages 10 to 13, found that "those 10 to 12 years old still very much want to be involved with their parents," says Dr. Alvin Poussaint, a Harvard Medical School psychiatry professor who helped interpret results. "I think parents might be surprised that children of this age are saying, 'We want to be close to you. We need you and we're still afraid. We need the sense of safety and security that you supply,'" Poussaint says.[6]

The five insights I have recommended can best be summed up by this wonderful poem. Read it to yourself and then to your child to let him or her know that you are there.

Tell Your Child, "I Am Here . . ."

I am here . . .

. . . to listen, not to work miracles.

. . . to help you discover what you feel, not to make the feelings go away.

. . . to help you identify your options, not to decide for you what you want to do.

. . . to discuss steps with you, not to take the steps with you.

. . . to help you discover your own strength, not to rescue you and leave you still vulnerable.

. . . to help you to choose, not to make it unnecessary for you to make difficult choices.

. . . to provide support for change.[7]

—Author Unknown

The third aspect of parent as hero is not expecting gratitude. Parents as heroes should not expect any type of major appreciation or recognition. Dale Carnegie, author and motivational speaker, openly discourages expecting gratitude. He wrote this about gratitude: "It is natural for people to forget to be grateful; so, if we go around expecting gratitude we are headed straight for a lot of headaches." His second point builds on the first. He says, "If we want to find happiness, let's stop thinking about gratitude or ingratitude and give for the inner joy of giving." And what should we expect from our children? Well, parents have been frustrated about the ingratitude of children for thousands of years. Can it be any different for your child? Dale Carnegie makes this final point: "Let's remember that gratitude is a 'cultivated' trait; so if we want our children to be grateful, we must train them to be grateful."

So how do you get gratitude? Kathryn Major explains the mystery of gratitude in another way: "Appreciation comes from the senses, but gratitude comes from the soul."

The fourth and last aspect of heroic parenting is that parents as heroes are decent. This means they are courteous, civilized, generous, respectable, and fair.

The woman behind me placed the book on the counter as I was finishing my transaction. As I walked away from the counter, my eyes spotted the first book she put down, it contained the phrase "Heroes and Greek Gods." Obviously "heroes" caught my eye. The woman asked the salesperson about a book at the counter regarding a basketball star. The woman picked up the book and asked, "Do you know anything about him?" The bookstore clerk responded with, "He is very popular." The woman replied, "Yes, but is he a decent human being?" The clerk said, "I really don't know."

I smiled as I walked out of the store. Decency. Yes, that is an important aspect of heroism. Is what the person doing decent?

Decency means displaying honesty, etiquette, righteousness, respectability, seemliness, in the general sense, acting appropriately.

In the 1992 movie *Hero* starring Dustin Hoffman, Geena Davis, and Andy Garcia, Garcia plays John Bubber. Bubber impersonates a hero who saved the lives of over 50 people in a plane crash. But the "fake" Bubber does offer the public some insight on heroes. In a news interview, Bubber says, "I think we are all heroes, if you catch us at the right moment. We all have something noble and decent in us trying to get out. And we are all less than heroic at other times. It is the media that notices one person one moment and not another. A hero is just a symbol of what is good in all of us."[8]

How do I keep going in all these four areas?

In *Hero,* John Bubber talks very softly to a boy in a coma in a hospital. Bubber tells the boy, "You're a hero. You can't quit. Heroes never quit."[9]

There are two Japanese proverbs that may prove helpful in enduring as a parent as hero. They are:

1. It is easier to rule a kingdom than to regulate a family.
2. Fall seven times, stand up eight.

Raising a family is a difficult and an unceasing responsibility. I think just realizing this fact will help in coping with your difficult task of raising your child. There will be days when you will "fall" but you need to tap your inner strength to cope with and overcome those struggling times. During those difficult parenting days and situations, keep going and keep trying.

A favorite children's story offers inspiration for parenting struggles. Remember the story of the "little engine that could"? It had always pulled small loads, but one day it had to tackle a much bigger one. Having a hard time getting the load to move at all, it encouraged itself by puffing, "I think I can, I think I can." The heavy load finally budged, and then momentum helped the little engine get it to the top of a hill. From that point on, the little engine had another helper, gravity, and it rolled smoothly downhill with its load, puffing happily, "I thought I could, I thought I could."

This story is often told to encourage a young person to try something that seems difficult, and it contains a great truth. To accomplish anything, we have to think and act as if we can. When we behave as if an undertaking is possible, existing laws come into effect to help us. When we reach the point of behaving as if the action were already accomplished, we receive even more help.[10]

You too can act as if you can. You can help your child perform better in school or cope with your child's illness or convey your love to your child. Start by acting as if you can.

Is it too late to help our children?

In today's society, children are experiencing many negative influences and stresses. Is it too late to help our children? Tama Murphy shared the story "White Horses" with me. The story was written in Tama's English class when she was 19. I think "White Horses" gives an appropriate warning to us all about helping our children.

Many years ago there was a quiet island just off the coast of England. It was covered with flowers, vines and other growing things and was very beautiful. The castle in the center of the island belonged to a lazy King. Around the castle, a herd of white horses ran free much to the King's delight.

The King would spend afternoons just watching the horses as they would run across the lovely island and play in the sea. The sea was held back by a wall that had seen many a year. Its once perfect line was now broken by a few rocks that had fallen out of place. The wall was neglected under the King's rule.

The King employed a wizard. When the wizard was young, he was very talented. As he got older he lost some of his power. However, once in a while he could perform a great deed. One day the King grew curious and asked the old wizard to create a crystal ball that could foretell the future.

After much work, the wizard created a gleaming crystal ball that he proudly presented to the King. The King was overjoyed and thanked the kind wizard for doing such a splendid job.

The lazy King placed the beautiful creation next to his bed. Then he waited for it to speak. Thinking of all the wonderful riches he might have in the future, the King began to dream of what he might hear. With his dreaming he hardly heard the ball say in a soft, but firm voice, "Soon." Looking at the crystal ball, the King pondered this for a short time, but soon forgot and went on his way.

The crystal ball did not speak for three years. Every day the maid would polish it for the lazy King. Many days went by when all the King would do was gaze at his lovely white horses. The herd grew in size, which pleased the King very much.

One day, before returning to bed, the King heard the crystal ball say in a loud, angrier voice, "Now." The King was a bit more concerned about the second message than the first but soon forgot and went about his pleasures.

Three more years passed and the land had remained just as fertile and prosperous as it had always been. The white horses still ran on the beaches and in the water. However, the King continued to neglect the wall that kept the sea from the island.

Then, one night, there was a terrible storm—worse than any they had seen. The furious wind uprooted the trees right out of the ground. As the King lay reading in his room, the crystal ball spoke again. It said in a creaking whisper, "Too Late."

An instant later the neglected wall fell into the swirling sea. The entire island was engulfed. All the people, and even the pretty white horses, drowned.

Even now you can see the memory of the white horses in the white caps of the waves. And, if you dive for mussels you can hear the bells of the drowned island ringing in the swell of the sea.

Get the message—don't procrastinate—we need to start NOW! The "soon" has already passed. We are at the now. Now is the time for parents to fulfill their role as hero, but they cannot do this alone.

Here is another story, Aesop's *The Bundle of Sticks* that illustrates that parents need support.

A certain man had several sons who were always quarreling with one another, and try as he might, he could not get them to live together in harmony. So he determined to convince them of their folly by the following means. Bidding them fetch a bundle of sticks, he invited each in turn to break it across his knee. All tried and all failed, and then he undid the bundle, and handed them the sticks one by one, when they had no difficulty at all in breaking them. "There, my boys," said he, "united you will be more than a match for your enemies: but if you quarrel and separate, your weakness will put you at the mercy of those who attack you." Union is strength.[11]

What does this mean? Parents can't do it alone. Schools can't do it alone. Raising our children means parents, schools, communities, houses of worship, government, and the media working together. Let me suggest two steps we need to take:

1. Each one of us needs to be awakened to the fact that we have an impact on the future of our children.
2. We need to work together. Regarding the first step, my major goal has been to remind parents of their major impact, hence this book. As mentioned in the beginning of the book, many parents believe they no longer have a major impact on raising their child. How untrue. I hope that from reading this book, you now understand the significance of your role as parent. Parents are not the only ones believing this fallacy of parents having little effect. Leaders in our communities are claiming that influence of parents is lessening.

I recently heard a priest talk about how the media has the biggest effect on our children. I was stunned. I went up to him after mass and asked him where he got his information. Was it from an article or a recent study? He looked at me and said, "Oh it was something I read many years ago and everyone knows this is still true." I smiled and left. I did not want to get into a major discussion on his error—yet. I decided I would send him a copy of my book and then talk to him about it. I know he will then have more up-to-date information and will be able to spread this needed gospel.

The second step—working together—begins with developing positive parenting and youth programs. The family has changed. Many times the family no longer has the support of two parents and an extended family. The family is no longer part of a close-knit community. We need something to assist in seeing and setting excellent parenting examples, uncovering positive role-models, and having support from individuals, groups, schools, and religious groups. There are already groups doing this such as the United Way, Focus On The Family, Family Resource Coalition, and Guideposts Family Information Network Database (FIND) but we need more.

Along with the creation of programs there needs to be publicity on the good things that are being done. The general public needs to learn about these developments. The media and government could help in this area. Again this is happening but in a fragmented way. Here are just a few of the good things happening:

- Michael Josephson developed the Josephson Institute on Ethics and established the Character Counts Coalition, which are teaching better ethical values to young people.

- Television and values: In a national poll of 750 10- to 16-year-olds, two-thirds of participants say that children their age are influenced by what they see on television. Four-fifths think TV entertainment shows should help teach children right from wrong.

Sixty-five percent of those polled find that programs such as "The Simpsons" and "Married . . . with Children" encourage a lack of respect for parents. And more than three-quarters think television portrays too much sex before marriage, with 62 percent stating that this influences young viewers toward early sex.[12]

The positive aspect of these findings is that our children know what is wrong with television and are communicating their concerns to adults.

• There are more and more people announcing who their role model is . . . parents. Comedian Rich Little made this statement: "Making my living as a comedian and an impressionist, I've learned that there's a difference between imitating someone for a laugh, and imitating someone as a way of life. You need to be very careful about who you choose to pattern your life after. And in my case there was nobody better to mimic than my dad."

• There is a trend towards recognizing the important task of raising and teaching our children. In Buffalo, New York, there is a celebration called "Heroes for a Modern Era." This event presents the Robert L. Wilson Award to a family, a school, and a community group that exemplify EPIC's (Effective Parenting Information for Children) commitment to children and families.

Conclusion

I believe the heroic criteria outlined in chapter 1 are not qualities and beliefs beyond your reach. In fact I think they are already an integral part of you but may need to be brought to the surface. As parent as hero, you have these attributes within you, it's a matter of bringing them to consciousness. And I hope I have assisted you in doing this. Worry less about the so-called media heroes and realize you are the highest of heroes to your child. Don't expect gratitude from your child or the community, just know you are doing a noble and worthwhile deed, one that cannot compare to any high sports salary or award-winning movie. This process of being a hero is a growth experience for you, your child, and society as a whole.

There are two major take-aways, that is, ideas I want you to remember.

1. You are your child's #1 hero and role model. I have said this over and over again. Understand you are your child's #1 hero and role model; know and share your values; strengthen your child's self-esteem and family-esteem; talk with your child and listen; and examine your child's environment. . . and be a major part of this environment.

Remember this:
- Parenting is difficult.
- Give each parenting situation a fair try.
- Act as if you are a hero.
- Now is the time to start fulfilling our commitment to youth.
- Union is strength.

2. You are also the interpreter and coach when it comes to heroes of today and yesterday.

- Point out positive traits and accomplishments from celebrities and sports stars.
- Discuss the good examples in mythology and history.
- There are many good people, helpers and courageous individuals in this world.
- As teenagers enter adulthood, they still need parents, mentors, and possibly coaches.
- But most of all, teens want to—and do—look up to parents as heroes, for support and for love.

I feel privileged to present this book to parents, honoring the many quiet heroes of our children. Raising children is one of the most difficult responsibilities anyone can have; it is also a special privilege. In a recent discussion with an elderly woman I told her how hard it is raising a child—the weariness, the anxieties, and frustrations of taking care of two children every day. She looked at me, with a tear in her eye, and told me that at least I have had this wonderful experience, as she will never know the specialness of such a relationship. It is an extraordinary opportunity, one we as parents may take for granted from time to time. Parents as heroes perform decent acts, endure, and amazingly enough find energy internally to fulfill this responsibility. Parenting is difficult yet rewarding.

Remember you are the fire, the major guiding light in your child's life. Congratulations, and keep up the good work, hero!

We must strengthen our commitment to model strong families ourselves, to live by godly priorities in a culture where self so often supersedes commitment to others. And as we not only model but assertively reach out to help others, we must realize that even huge societal problems are solved one person at a time.
—Charles Colson
American Author, Watergate Participant

Author's note

Heroes . . . and More Heroes

You have read about the profiles of the super stars, well-known individuals from the past, and the special teachers of our youth, but more important, you are now aware of the principles and responsibilities of parent as hero. I want to be more aware of the heroes in your child's life, particularly those demonstrating decency, perseverance, and generosity. By decency I mean appropriate and suitable behavior—words and actions that convey respect for your child, others, and society as a whole. Perseverance means persistence in pursuing a goal or dream. Perseverance also includes endurance, the ability to "hang on one minute longer." And generosity, of course, is being kind and sharing.

I'm looking for hints, methods, and examples of heroes in action—heroes who are parents, celebrities, Good Samaritans, and teachers—demonstrating decency, exhibiting endurance, and being unselfish. I want to pull together these people, stories, agencies that are providing positive change in youth. Whether it be in the form of a book, seminar, newsletter, "shareware," conference, computer bulletin board, or film, there is a place for this important bringing together of information and people.

Will you join me?

Write to me and tell me what decency, perseverance, and generosity are and tell me about the examples that you see, and also ideas on how to promote these values.

Write to:

TWS Resources
P.O. Box 492
Plattekill, New York 12568-0492

Appendix 1 for Chapter 1

Heroes in the Trimester of Life

Think of your life in three parts, that is divide your present age by three. For example, if you are 39 years old, there are three groups 1-13, 14-26, and 27-39.

Write down those individuals or characters that you saw or see now as heroes and why you consider them a hero. Is it because of their accomplishment, a certain characteristic or both?

Stage   Hero Admired   Attribute/Accomplishment

_____ _____   _____

_____ _____   _____

_____ _____   _____

_____ _____   _____

_____ _____   _____

_____ _____   _____

_____ _____   _____

Do this again with your child. You may first want to write down who you think are your child's heroes, and then have your child make a list. Try to be non-judgmental when your child shares this information with you—this is a time for you to learn about your child's heroes.

Appendix 2 for Chapter 2

Values In Real-life Situations

Think of a certain situation or circumstance that took place today. What values were involved? Did you display what you really felt? Is this the value you want to display to your child?

Situation _____

_____

List values (refer to lists in chapter 2) _____

_____

_____

Think about something your child did. What values were involved? Were you pleased with the behavior? If not, how can YOU better display this value for your child to see?

Situation _____

_____

Values displayed _____

What will you do differently?_____

_____

_____

Appendix 3 for Chapter 3

Building Family-esteem

       Which of the 30 activities are you doing now? Place an X next to these. Which activities do you want to start doing? Circle these activities. You have now created your Personalized Family-esteem Action Plan.

My family loves me.
1. Seek health for all family members.
2. Get physical.
3. Tell them, go ahead.
4. Be an athletic/activity supporter.
5. Reach out.
6. Pray with/for your child.

My family appreciates me.
7. Work on something together.
8. Get the value out of meals.
9. Clean up your act!
10. Think safety.
11. Do "a random act of kindness."
12. Write? Right!

My family has fun.
13. Get out!
14. Get reading.
15. Get fit.
16. Get going . . . on vacations.
17. Get in the picture.
18. Get nosy.

My family communicates.

19 Listen, listen, listen.

20. Be courteous in the family manner.

21. Don't make derogatory comments.

22. Keep everyone informed.

23. Shut off the TV.

24. Tell her/him about adult subjects before. . . .

My family life is balanced.

25. Remember your significant other and your parenting role.

26. Tell them what you do (and show them too).

27. Demonstrate your values within your family and community.

28. Wishin' and hopin'.

29. Have your own friends.

30. Get some QT . . . quiet time.

Appendix 4 for Chapter 4

Getting in Touch with Feelings

When talking and listening to your child it is helpful to talk about how your child is feeling. Here is a list of words to help you and your child get in touch with his or her emotions.

admired	afraid	alert	alive
amazed	amused	angry	annoyed
anxious	apprehensive	ashamed	attractive
awed	bashful	bitter	bored
cared-for	concerned	confused	content
critical	degraded	dejected	delighted
desperate	disappointed	discouraged	disgraced
edgy	embarrassed	empathetic	enthusiastic
excited	fed-up	frustrated	gloomy
graceful	great	happy	hopeful
horrified	hostile	humiliated	hurt
indifferent	inferior	joyful	lonely
loved	mad	mixed-up	panicky
patient	peaceful	popular	proud
rejected	relaxed	relieved	resentful
respected	sad	shocked	shy
strong	supported	sure	suspicious
sympathetic	tender	tense	threatened
trapped	trembling	uncertain	unloved
unpopular	unsure	upset	vibrant
warm	worthiness	worthy	zealous

Appendix 5 for Chapter 5

Guess Your Child's Favorite. . .

Make a list of your child's interest in the following items. Discuss these with your child.

	Your Answer	Child's Answer
Animal		
Book		
Candy		
Cartoon		
Color		
Dessert		
Food		
Friend or Classmate		
Fast Food		
Memory		
Movie		
Music Group		
Physical Activity		
Quiet Activity		
School Subject/Class		
Song		
Sports Team		
TV Show		
Video or Computer Game		
Wish List Item		

Appendix 6 for Chapter 6

Your Child's Most Favorite Individuals

List your child's ten most favorite celebrities. Hint: the best way to find this out is to ask him or her.

What are the accomplishments or traits that are appealing to your child?

Celebrity   Accomplishment or Trait

1 _____

2 _____

3 _____

4 _____

5 _____

6 _____

7 _____

8 _____

9 _____

10 _____

Appendix 7 for Chapter 7

Lessons from History and Mythology

List vacations, trips, and books you and your child have been involved with. What historical or mythological characters did you learn about? What lessons were detected?

     Vacation, Trip or Book   Lesson

1 _____

2 _____

3 _____

4 _____

5 _____

6 _____

7 _____

8 _____

9 _____

10 _____

Appendix 8 for Chapter 8

Keeping a Journal about Heroes

List three heroic people you or your child has heard about recently. Write down briefly what took place.

1 _____

_____

_____

2 _____

_____

_____

3 _____

_____

_____

Assist your child in starting a hero log or journal or book from newspapers and magazine clippings. Let your child decide what goes in the book.

Take time to brainstorm ideas with your child about what to put in the journal.

_____

_____

_____

_____

Appendix 9 for Chapter 9

Special People in Life

Create a list together with your child of teachers, seminar leaders, or others who did something special for you and your child. What did you learn?

Teacher, Mentor or Coach   What You Learned

1 _____

2 _____

3 _____

4 _____

5 _____

6 _____

7 _____

8 _____

9 _____

10 _____

Appendix 10 for Chapter 10

Life Plan for Growth

Develop a growth plan for you and your child by listing resources you will read and things you will do to help you and your child be a more decent person.

Your plan for development

Action Step   What You Learned

1 _____

2 _____

3 _____

4 _____

5 _____

6 _____

7 _____

8 _____

9 _____

10 _____

Your child's plan for development

Action Step   What You Learned

1 _____

2 _____

3 _____

4 _____

5 _____

6 _____

7 _____

8 _____

9 _____

10 _____

Notes

Chapter 1

1. *Webster's Ninth New Collegiate Dictionary*, Springfield, Mass.: Merriam-Webster, Inc., 1983, p. 566.
2. William Ecenbarger, "Mything in Action," *Chicago Tribune*, Chicago: July 5, 1992, pp. 20–22.
3. *Joseph Campbell and the Power of Myth with Bill Moyers, Program One: The Hero's Adventure*, New York: Mystic Fire Video, 1990.
4. Arthur Gordon, *Daily Guideposts 1993*, Carmel, N.Y.: Guideposts Associates Inc., 1992, p. 12.
5. *The State of America's Children Yearbook 1994*, Children's Defense Fund, 1994, Washington, D.C., p. 56.
6. Ibid.
7. Karen S. Peterson, "Speaking Out on the Need for Role Models," *USA Today*, September 13, 1993, pp. 1D-2D.
8. "Our Families . . . Our Future," Minneapolis, Minn.: Lutheran Brotherhood, p. 13.
9. Bill Sanders, *School Daze*, Grand Rapids, Mich.: Revell-Baker Book House, p. 168.
10. "What Influences Teenagers," *Parents & Teenagers*, April/May 1990, p. 5.
11. *Children Today*, November-December 1990, p. 31.

Chapter 2

1. "Do The Right Thing," *USA Weekend*, August 21-23, 1992, p. 6.
2. Sidney B. Simon, Leland W. Howe, Howard Kirschenbaum, *Values Clarification*, New York: Hart Publishing Company, Inc., 1978, pp. 291-92.
3. William J. Bennett, *The Book of Virtues*, New York: Simon & Schuster, 1993, pp. 21, 107, 185, 269, 347, 441, 527, 599, 665, 741.
4. *The Way to Happiness, A Common Sense Guide to Better Living*, Los Angeles, Calif.: The Way To Happiness Foundation, L. Ron Hubbard, Bridge Publications, Inc., 1989, pp. 7–21.
5. Norman Vincent Peale, *Seven Values To Live By*, Pawling, N.Y.: Peale Center for Christian Living, 1992, pp. 2–32.
6. Ibid.
7. *Life Application Bible*, The Living Bible, Wheaton, Ill.: Tyndale House Publishers, Inc., 1988, pp. 1800–1801.
8. Esme M. Infante, "Teens: Sex Can Wait For Wedding Bells," *USA Today*, July 29, 1994, p. 3D.

9. "A Report on the National Field Experiment to Assess the Impact of Human Sexuality: Values & Choices on Public School 7th and 8th Grade Youth," Values & Choices Research Summary, Minneapolis, Minn.: Search Institute, February, 1987, p. 3.

10. Thomas Leonard, "Tru Values Program," Coaching Forms Book, Salt Lake City, Utah: Coach University, 1994, pp. 2–3.

11. *Character & Destiny Application Guide*, Oak Brook, Ill.: Institute in Basic Life Principles, 1994, pp. 1–17.

12. Ibid.

13. Milton Rokeach, *The Nature of Human Values*, New York: The Free Press, a Division of Simon & Schuster Inc., 1973, pp. 7, 28.

14. "To Any Little Boy's Father," Og Mandino, *A Better Way to Live*, New York: Bantam Books, 1990, pp. 65–66.

15. Oscar Greene, *Daily Guideposts 1993*, Carmel, N.Y.: Guideposts Associates Inc., 1992, p. 139.

16. Arthur Gordon, *A Touch of Wonder*, Old Tappan, N.J.: Fleming H. Revell Company, 1974, pp. 225–27.

17. George H. Bierna, *Guideposts*, Carmel, N.Y.: Guideposts Associates Inc., January 1990, p. 21.

18. Norman Vincent Peale, *Daily Guideposts 1994*, Carmel, N.Y.: Guideposts Associates Inc., 1993, p. 125.

Chapter 3

1. Nathaniel Branden, Ph.D., *The Psychology of High Self-Esteem*, Chicago: Nightingale-Conant Corporation, 1986.

2. John R. Buri, Kathryn A. Hengel, Karen K. Komar and Lynda M. Richtsmeier, "An Arena of Comfort During Adolescence," *Student Self-Esteem: A Vital Element of School Services*, Garry R. Walz and Jeanne C. Bleuer, Ann Arbor, Mich.: Counseling and Personal Services, Inc., 1992, p. 286.

3. Jack Canfield, *Self-Esteem and Peak Performance*, CareerTrack Self-Esteem work book, Boulder, Colo.: CareerTrack Publications,1989, p. 7.

4. The California Task Force to Promote Self-Esteem and Personal Social Responsibility, "The Definition of Self-Esteem," *Student Self-Esteem: A Vital Element of School Services*, Garry R. Walz and Jeanne C. Bleuer, Ann Arbor, Mich.: Counseling and Personal Services, Inc. ,1992, pp. 27.

5. Garry R. Walz, "Counseling to Enhance Self-Esteem," *Student Self-Esteem: A Vital Element of School Services*, Garry R. Walz and Jeanne C. Bleuer, Ann Arbor, Mich.: Counseling and Personal Services, Inc., 1992, pp. 484-85. Ibid.

6. Weley R. Burr and Clark Christensen, "Undesirable Side Effects of Enhancing Self-Esteem," *Family Relations*, October 1992, pp. 460–64.

7. "Christopher News Notes," January 1994, No. 361, New York: The Christophers.

8. "Contact Newsletter," Dallas, Tex.: July, 1993.

9. "Quick Tips for Parents on Listening-Cooperation-Punishment," Albany, N.Y.: Federation on Child Abuse and Neglect.

10. Michael M. Omizo and Sharon A. Omizo, "The Effects of Participation in Group Counseling Sessions on Self-Esteem and Locus of Control Among Adolescents from Divorced Families," *Student Self-Esteem: A Vital Element of School Services,* Garry R. Walz and Jeanne C. Bleuer, Ann Arbor, Mich.: Counseling and Personal Services, Inc., 1992, p. 289.

11. C. E. Rollins, *52 Ways To Build Your Self-Esteem and Confidence,* Nashville, Tenn.: Thomas Nelson Publishers, 1992, p. 57–58.

12. Leonard Safir and William Safire, *Good Advice,* New York: Times Books, 1982, p. 291.

13. Kimberly Bittner, "Lost," *Sibling Information Network Newsletter,* The University of Connecticut, Vol. 9, No. 1,

Chapter 4

1. "Marriage Survey Results," *Today's Christian Woman,* March/April 1990, p. 32–34.

2. Dolores Curran, *Traits of a Healthy Family,* San Francisco: Harper & Row Publishers, 1983, p. 20.

3. "A New Switch—Teenagers Talk, Adults Listen," *The Christian Science Monitor,* July 21, 1994, p. 13.

4. Dawn Druly, "Thomas Gordon, The Effective Parent," *Parents,* December 1980, p. 47.

5. *Training Manual for HelpLine,* New York: HelpLine, pp. 38–41.

6. Kass Dotterweich, "Making Fresh Starts With Your Teen," St. Meinrad, Ind.: Abbey Press, 1988, p. 3.

7. "Building a Happy Home," *Christopher News Notes* No. 360, New York: The Christophers, December 1993.

8. "The Listening Art," *Christopher News Notes* No. 325, New York: The Christophers, May 1990.

9. Marion Bond West, *Daily Guideposts 1994,* Carmel, N.Y.: Guideposts Associates Inc. , 1993, pp. 191–192.

10. "Real Change Takes Initiative and Effort," *Poughkeepsie Journal,* July 3, 1994, p. 9A.

11. Denis M. Meade, Thomas G. Lynch, and Robert Fuller, "Adolescent Suicide," *Emergency Medical Services,* March 1995, p. 28.

12. J. Krishnamurti, submitted by David Spritzer, Israel, *Active Parenting Newsletter,* Atlanta, Ga.: Active Parenting, 1988.

13. "Plain Talk About . . . Adolescence," National Institute of Mental Health, DHHS Publication No. (ADM) 85-1065, 1985.

14. John Fax, "When Someone Deeply Listens to You," Contact of Chattanooga, March 1994, p. 3.

15. Dale Carnegie, *How To Win Friends and Influence People,* New York: Simon & Schuster, 1981, pp. 102–7.

16. Gary Smalley, *Hidden Keys to Successful Parenting,* Relationships Today, Inc., 1988, pp. 18-19.

17. Ibid.

18. Jennifer Lohrfink, "I'll Be Looking For You, Ace," *Guideposts,* Carmel, N.Y.: Guideposts Associates Inc., October 1987, pp. 38–39.

Notes

. Carol Kuykendall, *Daily Guideposts 1992*, Carmel, N.Y.: Guideposts Associates Inc., 1991, p. 211.

20. Kenneth L. Baldwin, "Give Children Love and Limits Instead of Lectures," *Poughkeepsie Journal*, October 23, 1994, p. 11A.

Chapter 5

1. Ann Beattie, *Picturing Will*, New York: Random House, Inc., 1989, p. 52.

2. "240 Ideas For Building Assets In Youth," Minneapolis, Minn.: Search Institute.

3. "The Troubled Journey: A Profile of American Youth," Minneapolis, Minn.: RespecTeen sponsored by Lutheran Brotherhood, pp. 1–13.

4. Ibid.

5. Ibid.

6. Ibid.

7. Ibid.

8. Ibid.

9. Leslie Ansley, "It Just Keeps Getting Worse," *USA Weekend*, Rockland Journal-News, August 13-15, 1993, pp. 4–6.

10. John Butterfield, "Teens and Drinking," *USA Weekend*, Poughkeepsie Journal, August 12-14, 1994, pp. 4–5.

11. The Journal of the American Medical Association, November 11, 1992 p. 2495.

12. Brenda Ling, "Parents Can Make A World of Difference," *USA Today*, December 15, 1993, p. 6D.

13. "Parents Dropping Out of Teens' Education," *Poughkeepsie Journal*, September 5, 1994, p. 1.

14. "240 Ideas For Building Assets In Youth," Minneapolis, Minn.: Search Institute.

15. *Christopher News Notes* No. 361, New York: The Christophers, January 1994.

16. "Focus on the Family with Dr. James C. Dobson," Colorado Springs, Colo.: Focus On The Family, November 1994, pp. 3–4.

17. Bob Demoss, "Focus on the Family With Dr. James C. Dobson," Colorado Springs, Colo.: Focus on the Family, August 1994, p. 3.

18. Bernard Cesarone, "Video Games and Children," ERIC Clearinghouse on Elementary and Early Childhood Education, University of Illinois, Urbana, January 1994, EDO-PS-94-3.

19. Meg A. Bozzone, "Spend Less Time Refereeing and More Time Teaching," *Instructor*, July/August 1994, pp. 88–91.

20. "How To Help Your Children Avoid Drugs," Williamsport, Pa.: Little League Baseball.

21. Dr. Michael H. Popkin, "Active Parenting Newsletter," Atlanta, Ga.

22. Gary Smalley and John Trent, Ph.D., *The Two Sides of Love*, Pomona, Calif.: Focus on the Family Publishing,1990, pp. 6–8.

23. *The Earthling*, Orion Pictures Corporation, 1980 Filmway Pictures.

24. "240 Ideas For Building Assets In Youth," Minneapolis, Minn.: Search Institute.

Chapter 6

1. *Forbes American Heritage,* American Heritage, a division of Forbes Inc., New York: January 1995, p. 80.

2. *The World Almanac and Book of Facts 1995,* New York: World Almanac, An Imprint of Pharo's Books, A Scripps Howard Company, 1994, p. 297.

3. Bill Sanders, *School Daze,* Grand Rapids, Mich.: Revell Baker Book House, p. 168.

4. *The World Almanac and Book of Facts 1992,* New York: World Almanac, An Imprint of Pharo's Books, A Scripps Howard Company,1991, p. 32.

5. *People Weekly,* New York: Time, Inc., December 26, 1994–January 2, 1995, p. 4.

6. *People Weekly,* New York: Time, Inc., September 19, 1994, p. 7.

7. *Good Housekeeping,* January 1995, p. 6.

8. *USA Today,* October 31, 1994, p. 1D.

9. Gary Smith, "Forty for the Ages," *Sports Illustrated,* 40th Anniversary Issue, Time, Inc., New York: September 19, 1994, pp. 49–146.

10. *USA Today,* October 24, 1994, p. 4D.

11. *USA Weekend,* November 18-20, 1994, p. 1.

12. *Readers Digest,* Pleasantville, N.Y.: The Readers Digest Association, Inc., January 1995, pp. 49-50.

13. Ibid.

14. Lawrence Kutner, "Heroes Offer Ways to Explore Feelings," *New York Times,* December 23, 1993, p. C5.

15. "Ministry of Money," Gaithersburg, Md.: Ministry of Money, 1989.

Chapter 7

1. "Poughkeepsie Journal TV Week," Poughkeepsie, New York: July 24—July 30, 1994, p. 2TV.

2. Maurice Saxby and Robert Ingpen, *The Great Deeds of Superheroes,* New York: Peter Bedrick Books, 1989, p. 7.

3. Charles Panati, *Extraordinary Origins of Everyday Things,* New York: Perennial Library, Harper & Row, 1987, pp. 416-17.

4. "Guiding The Choice of a Character to Emulate," *New York Times,* December 23, 1993, p. C5.

Chapter 8

1. *Times Herald Record,* Middletown, N.Y., August 1994.

2. Marjorie Eberts and Margaret Gisler, *Careers for Good Samaritans & Other Humanitarian Types,* Lincolnwood, Ill.: VGM Career Horizons, a division of NTC Publishing Group, 1991, p. 1–2.

3. Larry Margasak, "Heroes on the Spot," *USA Today,* October 31, 1994, p. 5A.

4. "1994 Salute to Public Servants" by the Editors of Federal Times, Army Times Publishing Company, April 2, 1994, p. 2.

5. "Heroes for Today," *Readers Digest*, March 1995, pp. 177–80.

6. "The Fourth Annual America's Awards," America's Awards, Pawling, N.Y., 1993.

7. John Ferro, "World Champ Next Door Nestles Up to New Paltz," *Poughkeepsie Journal*, June 9, 1991, p. 5F.

8. Ellen Stark, "The Top U.S. Charities," *Money*, December 1994, pp. 156–68.

9. Marjorie Eberts and Margaret Gisler, *Careers for Good Samaritans & Other Humanitarian Types*, Lincolnwood, Ill.: VGM Career Horizons, a division of NTC Publishing Group, 1991, pp. 118–19

10. Ibid., p. 116.

11. Norman Vincent Peale, "With Courage You Can Handle It," *Plus, The Magazine of Positive Thinking*, November 1986, p. 8.

12. Tamara Henry, "Up, Up and Out of Poverty," *USA Today*, July 25, 1994, pp. 1D–2D.

13. "The Community of St. Joseph at New Paltz Bulletin," July 17, 1994, St. Joseph Church, New Paltz, N.Y., p. 3.

14. Ace Collins, "Sunshine," *Plus, The Magazine of Positive Thinking*, March 1993, pp. 14–21.

15. Doris Toppen, "Ryan's Hope," *Plus, The Magazine of Positive Thinking*, July/August 1994, pp. 14–19.

16. Ibid.

17. Cliff Schimmels, "The Uninteresting Man From Smalltown, U.S.A.," *Guideposts*, May 1992, pp. 34–36.

18. Anita Manning, "Thousands Plan 'To Make A Difference," *USA Today*, October 21, 1994, p. 4D.

Chapter 9

1. Rebecca N. Saito and Dale A. Blyth of Search Institute, "Understanding Mentoring Relationships," July 1992.

2. Celia W. Dugger, "For Young, a Guiding Hand Out of Ghetto," *New York Times*, March 9, 1995, p. B12.

3. Carol Ascher, "The Mentoring of Disadvantaged Youth," New York: ERIC Clearinghouse On Urban Education, September 1988, No. 47, ISSN 0889-8049.

4. "A Tribute To Teachers: They've Made A Difference," *USA Today*, May 7, 1991, p. 6D.

5. Ibid., p. 7D.

6. Ibid., p. 6D.

7. "What Works, Research about Teaching and Learning," U.S. Department of Education, 1987, p. 46.

8. "Valued Youth: Potential Dropouts Serve as Tutors," Turning Points, Preparing American Youth for the 21st Century, Carnegie Council on Adolescent Development, Carnegie Corporation of New York, 1989, p. 47.

9. "Boys & Girls Clubs Names Texas Teen Youth of Year," *USA Today*, October 7, 1994, p. 6D.

10. Doug Levy, "Caring Parents Can Inspire Kids for College," *USA*

Today, February 21, 1995, p. 6D.

11. *The World Almanac and Book of Facts 1995*, New York: World Almanac, An Imprint of Pharo's Books, A Scripps Howard Company, 1991, p. 324–26.

12. Thomas Leonard, *Coaching Forms Book*, Salt Lake City, Utah: Coach University, 1994.

13. William J. Bennett, *The Book of Virtues*, New York: Simon & Schuster, 1993, p. 528.

14. Linda Ching Sledge, *Daily Guideposts 1994*, Carmel, N.Y.: Guideposts Associates Inc., 1993, pp. 218–19.

15. Becky Moser, "Mentors In Education," Knight-Ridder/Tribune News Service, June 1, 1994, p. 0601K6727.

16. "A Tribute To Teachers: They've Made a Difference," *USA Today*, May 6, 1992, p. 6D.

Chapter 10

1. Maurice Saxby and Robert Ingpen, *The Great Deeds of Superheroes*, New York: Peter Bedrick Books, 1989, p. 7.

2. David Elkind, "Teenage Idols," *Parents' Magazine*, January 1992, p. 117.

3. "Character Education," "What Works, Research about Teaching and Learning," Second Edition, United States Department of Education, 1987, p. 9.

4. Lynne S. Dumas, "Fallen Heroes," *Woman's Day*, February 21, 1995, p. 77.

5. Diane MacEachern, *Save Our Planet, 750 Everyday Ways You Can Help Clean Up the Earth* New York: Dell Publishing, 1992, p. IX.

6. Kim Painter, "Preteens Want To Be Close To Their Parents," *USA Today*, May 11, 1995, p. 1D.

7. "Contact of Knoxville Newsletter," Knoxville, Tenn.: April 1995, p. 1.

8. *Hero*, Columbia Pictures Industries Inc., 1992.

9. Ibid.

10. Three Gateways of Prayer, Unity, Unity Village, Mo., 1992, p. 46.

11. William J. Bennett, The Book of Virtues, New York: Simon & Schuster, 1993, p. 388.

12. "TV Values: Bart's Bad Influence," *Christian Science Monitor*, February, 28, 1995, p. 4.

Credits

For permission to reprint copyrighted material, grateful acknowledgment is made to the following authors and publishers:

- Information on pages 145 and 209-12 is reprinted with permission from *The World Almanac and Book of Facts 1995*. Copyright © 1994 Funk & Wagnalls Corporation. All rights reserved.

- Rokeach's Value Survey on pages 43-44 is adapted with the permission of The Free Press, a Division of Simon & Schuster Inc. From *The Nature of Human Values* by Milton Rokeach. Copyright © 1973 by The Free Press.

- Excerpt on page 135 from *The Two Sides of Love* by Gary Smalley and John Trent, Ph.D., published by Focus on the Family, is copyright © 1990, 1992. Used by permission.

- Information on pages 115, 125, and 137 is reprinted with permission from *240 Ideas for Building Assets in Youth*. Copyright © 1994 by Search Institute, Minneapolis, Minn.; 1-800-888-7828. All rights reserved by Search Institute.

- Information on pages 116-21 is reprinted with permission from *The Troubled Journey*, by Dr. Peter L. Benson. Copyright © 1993 by Search Institute, Minneapolis, Minn.; 1-800-888-7828. All rights reserved by Search Institute.

- Character training information on pages 41-43 is reprinted from *Character and Destiny*. Used by permission of the Institute in Basic Life Principles, May 1995.

- *Picturing Will* by Ann Beattie, is copyright © 1989 by Random House, Inc., New York. Excerpt on page 114 is reprinted with permission.

- Excerpt on page 155 from "Exposing the Myth of the Generation Gap" by Everett C. Ladd, (*Reader's Digest*, January 1995) is reprinted by permission. Copyright © 1994 by the Reader's Digest Assn., Inc.

- Information on pages 38-39 is reprinted with permission from Technical Report of the National Demonstration Project Field Test of Values and Choices, by Michael J. Donahue, Ph.D. Copyright © 1987

Index